The Blessings of Miniature Baseball

Craig Martin Barnes

World rights reserved. This book or any portion thereof may not be copied or reproduced in any form or manner whatever, except as provided by law, without the written permis-sion of the publisher, except by a reviewer who may quote brief passages in a review, or as specifically stated in this book.

The author assumes full responsibility for the accuracy of all facts and quotations as cited in this book. The opinions expressed in this book are the author's personal views and interpretations, and do not necessarily reflect those of the publisher.

This book is provided with the understanding that the publisher is not engaged in giving spiritual, legal, medical, or other professional advice. If authoritative advice is needed, the reader should seek the counsel of a competent professional.

Copyright © 2016 Craig Martin Barnes
ISBN-13: 978-1-4796-0552-1 (Paperback)
ISBN-13: 978-1-4796-0552-1 (ePub)
ISBN-13: 978-1-4796-0554-5 (Mobi)
Library of Congress Control Number: 2015913732

Published by

Acknowledgements

To our heavenly Father for the inspiration, thus making it fun; to my wife and my parents (not necessarily in that order) for putting up with this all these years, thus making it possible; and to our next door neighbor for making all this necessary.

And finally, one last tribute before I get off the soapbox. I had asked Minnie Miñoso to write a foreword to my book. But alas! To my heartbreak, I am not sure he received it in time to actually read it, for he passed away about the time it was due to arrive.

For me, Saturnino Orestes Armas (Arrieta) ("Minnie") Miñoso was an example to youngsters growing up of how to "play the game," both on and off the field—in sports and in the "game of life." He encouraged youth to put God, family, and homework all ahead of baseball; and then, when on the field, to not slack off, but to put forth every effort constantly, because those who pay good money to watch you play deserve to get what they paid for. And when you think about it, you don't have to be a baseball player for that to count.

So, in memoriam, I present my request to him in my exact words:

Mr. Miñoso,

All my life you have been my all-time favorite player. I was angry when they traded you to Cleveland. I was deliriously happy when you were traded back. I was upset again when they traded you to St. Louis and figured that, had you been in Chicago, you would not have been injured (VBWG). And the only time in my whole life I have ever cheered against my favorite team was when I saw you hit a homerun when you were playing for Washington. As I remember, I was one of many who cheered for you that day. I also remember thinking when you stepped into the box, "Wouldn't it be cool if you hit a homerun right now?" And sure enough!

I still remember the play vividly—the ball arching into the left-field stands, and watching you trot past me between third base and home plate. What a thrill for a fourteen year old!

All my life I heard my mother tell me what her father would say about you, "Minneapolis Minnesota (referring to you), the pitchers better watch out for him. He [sic] bad medicine." I don't know whether you remember this, but I remember one time (and my mother talks about this a lot, too) when both teams left the dugouts to participate in an "attitude adjustment social occasion." You sat down on second base rather than participate in the fisticuffs. I don't know how your teammates felt about that, but your stock with me soared! One time, when I was visiting Cooperstown, I was touched with thoughts about you. Where is Minnie's plaque? Why is there not a plaque for him? And I began thinking, if they are considering only your major league career, you will be cut short because you had a late start in the majors. So, I hope you don't mind, but I put in the suggestion box that they need to consider your pre-majors career, also (not to mention your post-majors career). Your whole career. And you know what? The next thing I knew (it seems like it was within a year) they put you on the Negro Leagues ballot. But, alas! Still no induction. I have no doubt it will happen, but I want to see it happen while you are still around to enjoy it.

As such, I would be honored if you would be willing to write the foreword to my book.

****

So, my friend, even though we never formally met, thank you so very much! Sadly, we will miss your foreword. However, your life is a personification of what I want to do with this book, and your legacy lives on in the people you have encouraged, and, in turn, in the people they influence …

Sincerely,
Craig Martin Barnes
A "satisfied customer"

Contents

Foreword 7

Preface 8

Introduction 10

Chapter 1   The Walk-Off Foul Ball 12

Chapter 2   The Basic Field Game. 16

Chapter 3   "Fundamentals"—Technical Issues 44

Chapter 4   A "Level" Playing Field 56

Chapter 5   The Commissioner's "Antics"—Administrative Considerations . . . 69

Chapter 6   You Be the Boss—Other Versions 73

Chapter 7   Play Ball! 77

Appendix A   Know the Score (The Scoresheet). 78

Appendix B   Dead Ringer and Ambidextrous Persons. 79

Appendix C   The Lineup Selection Worksheet 82

Appendix D   The Stake Out (Instructions for Setting-up the Default Lines) . . 87

Appendix E   Oops! (Remedial Options for Errant Play on the Field) 94

Index 96

Foreword

Having enjoyed firsthand the small ball game, I can say with conviction how much fun it is! I have been involved as a player or coach all of my life in the game of baseball. I have experienced the game at every level from little league all the way to the Major Leagues. Small ball gives players of all abilities the opportunity to participate and succeed in the game of baseball. The unique design offered by Pastor Barnes of the field, as well as the rules, levels the playing field in so many ways.

The beauty and integrity of the game is masterfully preserved in small ball, while allowing a smaller amount of players with varied ability to compete against each other. The joy I have experienced on the field for many years is evident with the participants of this game, the agony is there as well. I strongly encourage you to give this game a try, get outdoors and enjoy God's masterpiece. Just watch out for ambidextrous pastors with wicked knuckle balls if you are ever in Middle Tennessee.

Scott Willcutt
Pegram, TN

Preface

The Default Lines

This illustration is in the public domain. You may copy it, give it to your friends, and use it for playing games, etc. Available at: http://glorylight.org/MiBaseball_Field_Plan.jpg or http://1ref.us/field Have fun!

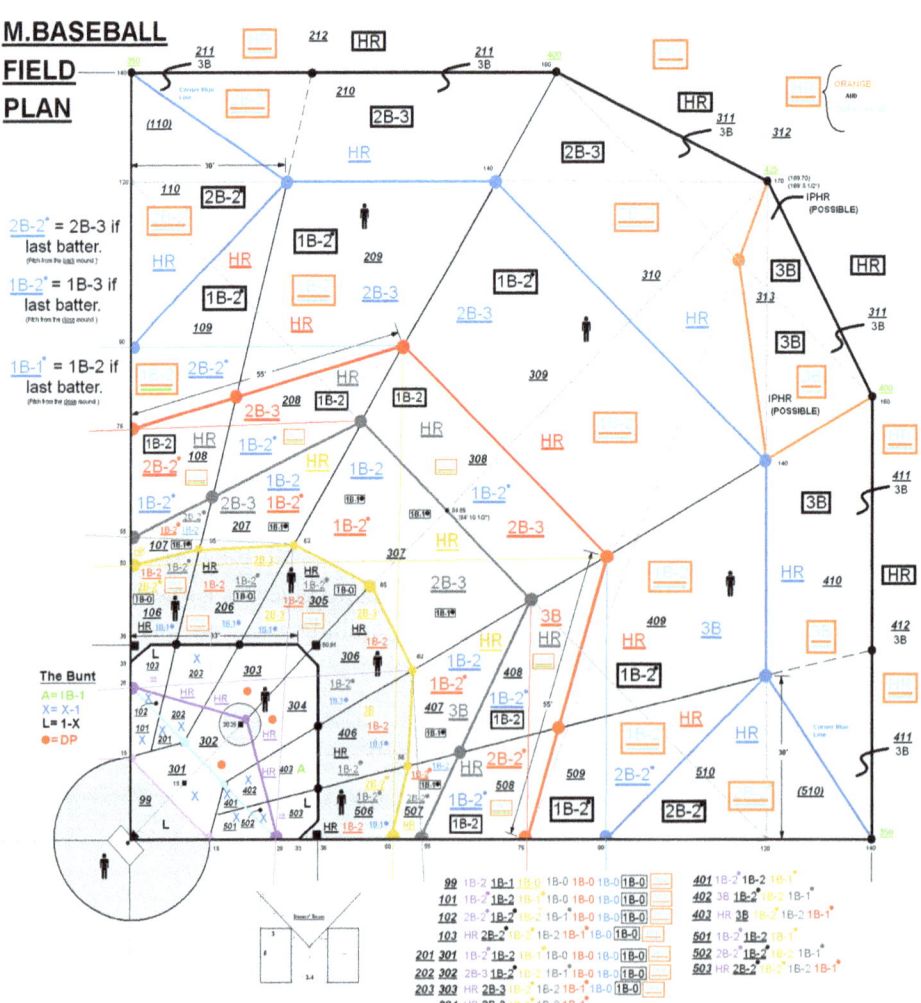

A Modified Black Line Superimposed

(Illustration: Not to be used in a game.)

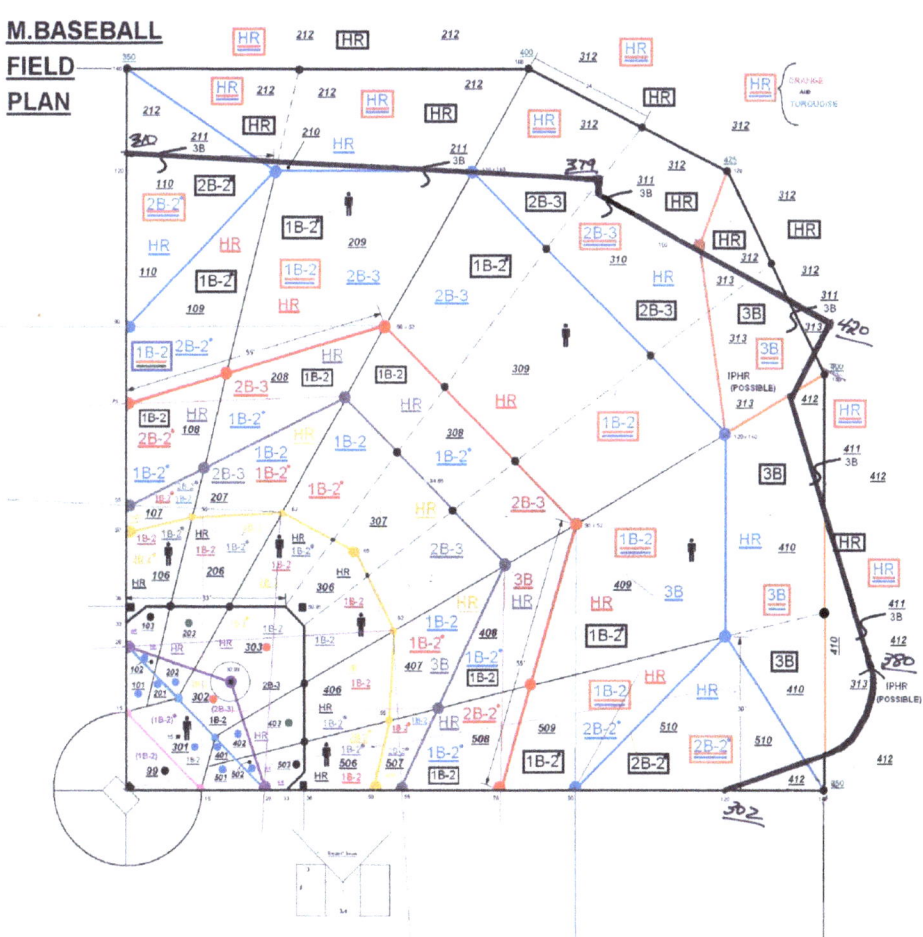

Introduction

Why would a pastor write a book about baseball? Well, first, maybe because it is something one can do outside in the fresh air, thus improving one's health? Maybe because it is educational, thus improving one's life? Maybe because, as serious as life can get, he likes to see people have some fun? Maybe because he just likes the game? For me, it is all of these things, but there is even more.

I am taking a break from my more serious writing to bring to you a concern I have had for many years. The benefits of playing baseball carry over to life in general and can have an everlasting impact on the developing personality of young people and their families. How can I find a way for serious fans of baseball to have a new opportunity to play, and even for those who just like to play out of doors to have an opportunity to play something that they have never played before? Not everyone can play 9" hardball or even 12" softball. There are millions of people who, for one reason or another, cannot play these games. Usually, the reasons are human, such as physical strength, balance, agility, ability to run, age, or basic skill level. Other reasons pertain to time and space restraints or even the number of people available to play.

Miniature baseball is a game played on a 40 percent scale size regulation baseball field. The exceptions are the pitcher's distance, which is 30 feet 3 inches (50 percent) and the batter's boxes. Any question about whether you can expect true performance and returns to scale is obliterated with the first pitch.

For example, the 5" balls can occasionally travel in excess of 200 literal feet (or 500 scale feet). The longest ball ever hit had a tailwind and was measured at 296 literal feet (or

740 scale feet). It hit about 40 feet up in a pine tree and dropped straight down, where it stopped. It was measured from there. The modern record is 273 literal feet (683 scale feet) with no noticeable tailwind. The 5" ball will support fastballs, curve balls, sliders, a variety of change-ups, fork balls, cutters, knuckleballs, etc., and are available to pitchers via standard grips and wrist motions. Most overhand fastballs range between 40 and 50 miles per hour (mph) (80 to 100 scale mph, calculated on a pitching distance of 30 feet, 3 inches). However, depending on the pitcher, speeds can range in excess of 70 mph (140 scale mph). The fastest clocked pitch was 81 mph (162 scale mph). The initial reaction from most people upon first encountering this game is that they will never be able to hit such a small ball, but they are soon surprised!

In this book, I propose an alternative that will allow millions of people who long to play an invigorating (but not exhausting) game in the fresh air of God's creation[1] to be able to participate on a competent level in the greatest game ever created—baseball.

Play ball!

---

[1] Playing in a smoggy city might erode this goal somewhat, but I'm guessing that smoggy outdoor air is still better than stale indoor air. We do the best we can in the circumstances provided us.

Chapter 1

The Walk-Off Foul Ball

October is the great time of year,[2] for while the weather is cooling, this is the time when exciting things begin heating up. Even the leaves brighten in anticipation of what is about to happen, for this is the season of the post season. Today is the seventh game of the World Series!

The "heat" is on and the trees look as if they are on fire!

This year's series is tied at three games apiece. The White Fox have a 4 to 1 lead with the Dragonflies batting in the bottom of the tenth inning. The White Fox have their ace closer Lefty Samson facing the Dragonflies' mighty Witey Casey at the bat. The bases are loaded and Witey is the final batter of the game. Everything that has happened the whole year has come down to this moment. It is now or never.

Lefty guns the ball toward home plate. However, Witey is undaunted, so he takes a mighty swing and launches a bomb down the left field line. Mayhem breaks loose as everyone is shouting, waving, and blowing at the ball, trying to force it either fair or foul depending on whether you favor the White Fox or the Dragonflies. I must say, that poor ball is taking quite a beating. However, the ball is foul by inches—but not foul enough.[3]

"What are you doing?"

---

[2] Next to spring, of course, which is the start of baseball season.
[3] "Right size, wrong shape," Ken "Hawk" Harrelson.

An eerie hush descends upon the ball field. No one is breathing. No one dares to move as the weather takes a sudden turn toward frigid. As a result, everyone is frozen in place, and in your mind's ear you can hear the crack of icicles falling to their deaths. The neighbor is shouting now. "How many times have I told you not to hit baseballs into my petunias?"

Oh boy! Not again!

"Well! This ball is mine!" And she struts back into the house—with our only ball! Everyone goes home. Of all things! A walk-off foul ball!

****

Has this ever happened to you? If you ever were a youngster growing up in a big baseball suburb as I did, probably so. Maybe not exactly as this hokey fictitious illustration reveals, but it did happen that we outgrew our backyard—and we did lose balls to our next door neighbor. Finally, we concluded that we were not going to get any younger, nor were we likely to lose strength as we aged.[4]

There was a park across the street, but even that was not big enough for a regulation baseball field. I still remember the day we were playing in that park and I hit a baseball into a passing dump truck! Yes, this really did happen. Who knows how many miles that ball went before it finally hit the ground! Needless to say, it was unanimously declared a homerun. And it was the walk-off variety at that, for it was indeed our only ball. However, it was kind of scary. What if that ball had hit the windshield instead of the cargo bin? You know, I think I prefer petunias.

Alas, another baseball field down the drain. What to do?

But that was not all. There was another issue. Except for Little League, which only played once a week, we never ever had 18 total players to make up a real, self-respecting, organized baseball game. We played on "half-field" slivers—yuk! So much for going with the pitch. Again, what to do?

I believe God gave us the answer.

We invented miniature baseball. No more broken windows. No more crushed petunias. No more risk of injury or angry neighbors. You could now hit a baseball directly at a nearby house without worry. And even if a batted ball did hit the house (or even the windows!) with full force, there was no damage. Yay! Hurrah! Our backyard was now big enough!

A new era had begun.

Miniature baseball received its beginnings from the broken window, fortunately, the only one we ever broke. There is nothing like coming into the kitchen to prepare the evening meal only to find a baseball entrenched in your kitchen sink buried under a layer of broken glass! That will enhance your appetite! Instead of getting angry with us, my

---

4   Bear with me on this. Now that I am a senior citizen, I have a different perspective. (By the way, even at my age I can still average a homerun about once every ten at bats, depending on the pitching.)

parents were philosophical about it. I think they thought it was funny, even though they never overtly expressed that sentiment. I was under the impression that they had been wondering how long it was going to take for us to outgrow our backyard.[5] That's when we began to seriously seek a solution to our dilemma—miniature baseball was now in its embryonic form.

****

Baseball is a spiritual game. You do not reach your highest level of performance through selfishness. You need communication with your heavenly Father to reach His best performance in you. Yes, even though those blood and guts, bumps and bruises, crash, clash, boom, bang games are macho and even exciting at times, they cannot hold a candle to the spirituality of baseball. After all, how many brains does it take to bash the person next to you as hard as you possibly can?[6] However, the first three rules of baseball are 1) concentrate, 2) concentrate, and 3) concentrate. Know where the fielders are and their individual abilities for both teams, and in any situation. Know what the opposing (and your own) pitchers and batters can do. A bunt can be more effective than a homerun in certain situations. You need to know your own skills, how to stay within your ability, and how to compensate and be willing to adjust. You need to know what to do with the ball when you get it. Keep a short swing. Don't overthrow. Move the runners over. You need "soft hands."

Remember, a pitch thrown without conviction goes a long way![7]

Be willing to sacrifice your own glory for the benefit of your team—for each of the players. The best teams know each other, what their strengths and weaknesses are, and how to make adjustments for each other—during the game, and also off the field—without being condemnatory. This is what baseball is all about. Everyone should learn how to play baseball (or one of its derivatives) at some time in their lives. In my opinion, raw skills mean a lot, but when it is all said and done, and the leaves fall off the trees in boredom, the team that carries home the trophy with all those flags is the team that concentrated and self-sacrificed the most.[8]

I call all this "the will to succeed."

Miniature baseball carries many, if not most, of the spiritual benefits of softball and regular hardball without needing a large space, without needing more than two total players to play a game,[9] and without risk of injury. Even throwing at hitters means nothing!

---

5 I am still thankful it wasn't me that hit the ball that broke the window, even though I never feared my parents wrath over that. I had good, understanding parents, and I knew it.
6 I'm not naming any sports here.
7 In contrast, a prayer said without conviction doesn't rise above the ceiling.
8 Not to be confused with the sacrifice bunt.
9 Although eight total players is ideal.

Don't be deceived. Softballs are not soft! They are just bigger. I can tell you horror stories of injuries acquired during "soft"ball games. [10]

****

When I was a child, I was sent to the tennis courts almost every day. You only need two total players to play that game, you know, but four is even better because that involves at least a little teamwork. But tennis made me feel guilty. After all, how much fun is it when every time you ace a serve, it is a "called strike three"? Or when you hit the ball over the fence on the fly—Yay! A homerun! A majestic thing of beauty!—but you get penalized for it anyway? And when you hold serve, you "got out of the inning" without giving up a run, and when you break serve (Wow!), you just put a crooked number up on the scoreboard! "Hey, hey!" "Holy cow!" "You can put it on the booooooard—yes!"[11] That is what tennis was for me.

We actually invented another game called "tennis golf" where, among other things, one of the "holes" required us to hit tennis balls across a crowded swimming pool. (Again, a majestic thing of beauty. Two fences to hit the ball over!) Talk about more dangerous than a sand trap! You had to be really careful! One mistake here and YOU might become the object of *the* "grand slam"! (This was when we were supposed to be playing tennis.) The funny thing is, we never got in trouble for doing that.[12] But that is the subject for another book.[13]

Seriously, every time I finish playing an exciting game of miniature baseball (and it seems like they are almost always decided by one run or less[14]), as I leave, I pause to look over the field and thank God for giving me this game. After all, there are no losers.

I pray the same can happen for you.

---

10   Sixteen-inch softballs are the biggest balls I have ever played with, and they do become soft with use; but when new, they can be very hard also. It's like a rock coming at you—and we played without gloves!
11   For those of you who may not know, these are quotes from Jack Brickhouse, Harry Caray, and Ken "Hawk" Harrelson, respectively.
12   I guess that is because we were always successfully "really careful."
13   Please don't get me wrong. Tennis is a great sport; it just wasn't my first love.
14   Actually, in the last 16 games played before this writing, games decided by 1 run=10; 2 runs=2; 3 runs=2; 4 runs=2.

Chapter 2

The Basic Field Game

      These rules modify official Major League Baseball rules. If not covered by these rules, except for matters of clothing and equipment, the official Major League Baseball rules are to be applied using the latest version available.

      Having said this, I have one general note about the rules of my favorite game. Rules, by definition, are not perfect. The concept may be perfect, but the human application of a perfect concept is going to be flawed this side of eternity. However, there are a number of baseball rules that, in my opinion, if adjusted, would probably increase fairness and reality. I greatly hail the instant replay that Major League Baseball began to incorporate in 2014. What an improvement! Oh how I hated those arguments where the managers felt they had to defend their teams from the "attacks" by the umpires. Yay! Carry on! I support the eventual expansion of the instant replay to balls and strikes.[15] I understand the technology is nearly available even for that, if not already here.[16]

****

---

15   The umpire would still have the final say, but if he could hear a beep, he would be greatly assisted.

16   In miniature baseball (and, as far as I know, only in miniature baseball, can this be practical without electronic assistance), the baskets accomplish much of this enhancement.

As a means of introducing the miniature baseball modifications of official Major League Baseball rules, recommended game adjustments are listed below in order of the level of descending illogicalness, the top being the most illogical of the current rules (and also the easiest to fix):

- **The Infield Fly Rule** – Make the fielder catch the ball. When the umpires call the fly ball rule into play, the batter is safe at first base and no runners are forced out at the next base if the fielder drops it. I recommend extending this to all fly balls, including those in the outfield.[17]

- **The Automatic Double** – Give the batter the benefit of the doubt for hitting the ball over the fence, even if it is on the bounce. Award three bases to the runners and a triple or a double depending on where the ball went out of play—in fair or foul territory respectively.[18]

- **The Hit by Pitch** – If the catcher catches the ball (as in a foul tip—not as in a pop up), the batter was not hit. This should eliminate a lot of confusion.

- **Extra Innings** – Save on your pitchers—restrict extra innings to one tiebreaker inning.[19]

- **Fan Interference** – Let the fan play the game as long as no part of the fan's feet touches the ground in play.[20]

---

17 Line drives happen so quickly that there is no time to call the fly ball rule. Therefore, the rule would not apply to line drives.
18 This has indeed been incorporated into the miniature baseball rules. (By the way, one person I've talked to believes that a ball bouncing over the fence should be a homerun.)
19 Besides, some of us older ones have to go to bed at night. If you know this is the deciding inning, who is going to turn the TV off? (See below for a sample of how the tiebreaker is done in miniature baseball.)
20 Treat the ball touching the fan the same as touching an umpire; the ball is in play as if not touched. However, if the fan catches it and pulls it over the fence, or if he throws it, it's gone. Note: Should the fan go after the player instead of the ball, you have a different situation.

- **The Designated Hitter** – Let the pitcher bat in the lineup and let the DH bat for anyone, as a manager option for game situations, and under certain circumstances. (This would enhance specific game situations and would also tend to increase runs per game.)[21]

- **The Mound** – Raise the mound to a prior era level (for the safety of the pitchers). (This would tend to decrease runs per game.)[22]

- **Collisions at the Plate** – I don't necessarily recommend this last rule. However, if we ever want to truly eliminate collisions at the plate, we will probably need to remove the requirement to tag the runner trying to score, once the runner has passed the halfway point between third base and home plate.

My recommended scoring changes are as follows:

- **Team Errors** – "Somebody should have caught it."

- **Wins** – Give the starter the win if he leaves the game after 5 innings with his team ahead and also his team eventually goes on to win regardless of whether the lead changes after he departs.

- **Saves** – Charge the pitcher who actually closes the game with a "scare" if his team wins after the lead changes while he is pitching—while still applying the other save rules. For example, if he blows the save and his team goes on to win, charge him with a scare, and not the win, if he is the last pitcher for his team. (The win would go to the pitcher who, under concurrent rules, would have received the win had the save been successful to begin with.)

- **Double Play Error** – Allow the error on either end of a potential double play, assuming the out should have been made with a good play. An exception might be on the throw from second base because of contact with the runner.

- **Earned Run Average** – When a pitching change is made with runners on base, divide any earned runs into three parts and charge the various contributing

---

21 Don't think for a minute this will not add excitement to the game. Babe Ruth coming to bat with the bases loaded? *You* would have to be loaded to not get caught up in that! This should be good in (and satisfy the proponents of) either league, since the pitcher is still present to bat. (Notes: The DH bats for different players as needed. The player being batted for would not be required to be replaced. Other restrictions also apply, such as how often you can bat for the same player. In simulated games using this rule, the DH really does not bat nearly as often as one would think; and no, he does not bat every inning—maybe three to five times during the game.)

22 I have a major concern for the pitchers. They seem to be more injury prone, and their arms take a terrible beating! Pitching is so important for the success of a team. It is a huge investment, only to have a pitcher end up on the disabled list. By the way, in miniature baseball this is not an issue. Pitchers can pitch the whole game every day. What generally prevents that from happening is either time restraints or other players who also like to pitch. (What a surprise!)

pitchers with the bases actually given up to contribute to the earned run. This would have a tendency to optimize the earned run average between starters and relievers.

- If there are 2 outs when the pitching change is made:
  - Runner on 3rd base: 2/3 for the old pitcher, and 1/3 for the new pitcher.
  - Runner on 2nd base: 1/3 for the old pitcher, and 2/3 for the new pitcher.
  - Runner on 1st base: none for the old pitcher, and 3/3 for the new pitcher.
- If there are less than 2 outs when the pitching change is made:
  - Runner on 3rd base: 3/3 for the old pitcher, and none for the new pitcher.
  - Runner on 2nd base: 2/3 for the old pitcher, and 1/3 for the new pitcher.
  - Runner on 1st base: 1/3 for the old pitcher, and 2/3 for the new pitcher.

I have tried to incorporate as many of these changes as practical into the miniature baseball rules. The specific applications of some of these can be seen in this book. The rest of this chapter is dedicated to additional rule changes.

The Field

- As mentioned earlier, miniature baseball is a game played on a 40 percent scale size regulation baseball field. The exceptions are the pitcher's distance, which is 30 feet 3 inches (50 percent) and the 3-foot by 5-foot batter's boxes, which are illustrated below. There is a second "mound" (or "plate") that is 15 feet from home plate, which is used for "base running" considerations. Neither plate needs to be raised.[23] The fences can be as small as logs or utility poles stretched out on the ground or can be scaled to 40 percent if modeling a prototypical baseball field, such as Fenway Park with its "Green Monster" in left field.

---

23   Except for, possibly, drainage purposes.

The Equipment

- The equipment is designed to be safe for the players and spectators. The only injury I am ever aware of in the last 50 years happened when I received a bloody nose because I was standing too close to the batter.[24]

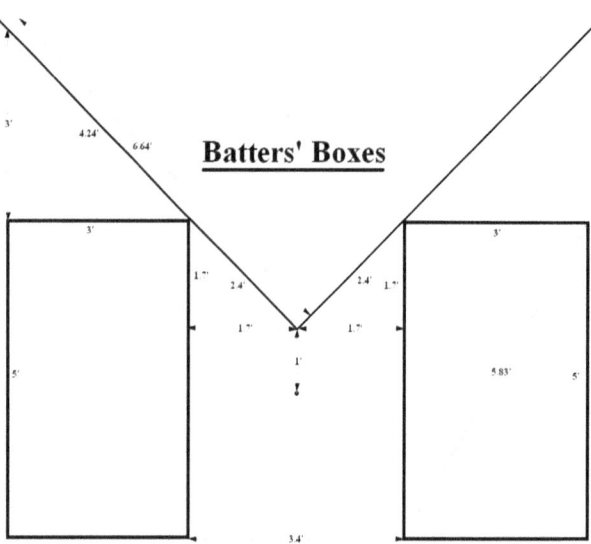

---

24 This was during a time when we sometimes allowed the pitchers to pitch from 15 feet. Did I leave the game? Are you kidding?

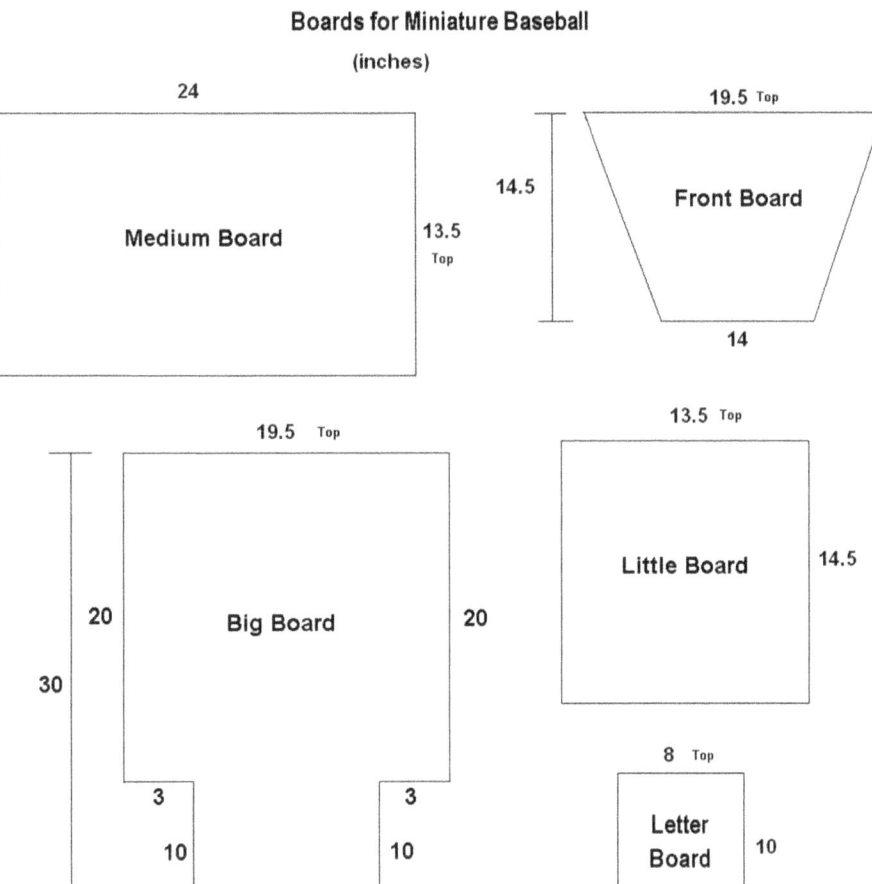

- Balls – Plastic golf balls:
  - White – firm,[25] no holes,[26] weighted with cloth to ½ ounce or 14.1745 grams.
  - Orange – firm, with holes, weighted with orange cloth to ½ ounce or 14.1745 grams.
  - Turquoise – soft,[27] with holes, weighted with turquoise or blue cloth to ½ ounce or 14.1745 grams. These are used for specific handicaps.

---

25 Does not depress when squeezed.
26 Except the hole needed to insert the cloth.
27 Can be depressed when squeezed.

- Bats – Thin, plastic "Official Wiffle Bat,"[28] and a fat plastic bat[29] for some types of tee shots.
- Laundry baskets – rectangular, standard size (2).
- Strike Zone Boards (shown above) – ¼-inch plywood or other type board.
- Tee – The ball can be supported by pipe insulation of various lengths.
- Ancillary balls – Up to 3 plastic 9" baseballs or wiffle balls of the same size (optional) and a plastic 12" softball, if available.
- Can – an empty #10 can.

Players

- Eight total players are ideal; however, the game can accommodate 2 to 12 total players. The ages of the players can be old enough for their mothers to feel sufficiently comfortable to place their bassinets in the batter's box until they can no longer sit in a wheel chair. Realistically, more like ages 5 to 95, depending on the individual. This game encourages participation of both ladies and gentlemen in the same game, for it is the type of game that allows all to fully participate. (For brevity I am not going to type "he/she" every time the situation arises. Please accept "he" as a universal reference.)

However, before I talk to you about our players, I would like to introduce you to our good friend, Dead Ringer, which is used to even the sides.

- **"Dead Ringer"**
  - The game can be played with any number of players from 2 to 12 (1 to 6 per side), with an invisible player named "Dead Ringer" who adjusts the teams if there is an odd number of human players or if there is a shortage of players to reach the preferred quantity of 4 players per side.
    (See chapter 5 for more information on Dead Ringer, absent players, and trying for a tee shot.)
- **"Person" vs. "Player" – the ambidextrous "Two-player Person"**
  - The ambidextrous player can be a huge help to the scorekeeper in providing flexibility for making the lineups because he provides an extra "player" to use, if needed. This is particularly true when using the Random Roster Program.

---

28 The Wiffle Ball, Inc., 275 Bridgeport Avenue, P.O. Box 193, Shelton, CT 06484. Phone: (203) 924-4643. FAX: (203) 924-9433.
29 Referred to in this book as the "Orange Bat," but it can be any color.

A "player" is an entry on the roster. A "person" (or, in the plural, "people" or "persons") is a living breathing human being. The same person can represent more than one player in the league if each player both bats and throws differently.[30] For example, "Witey" bats and throws right handed and "Lefty" bats and throws left handed. Both players must be pitchers[31] to qualify for this status. A person who elects to do this cannot also play as a regular player (using his or her regular name). Whenever he plays, he plays as either "Lefty" or "Witey" (or both, as two players in the same game) and if he starts the season playing as a regular person (and vice versa), he should only change to ambidextrous once during the whole season. This does not preclude a switch hitter (or a switch pitcher) from being able to do the switching as a regular player.[32] It only affects playing as two players, especially as it relates to playing as such in the same game.

It is easiest if both players play on the same team, but this is not necessary. Therefore, the possibility that they might have to "face" each other does exist, in which case one of the players either hits off the tee or pitches to an absent batter. In my opinion, it is best to use your ambidextrous players as an alternative to (but not a "substitute" for) using Dead Ringer whenever you can. Everything else being equal, have them play on the same team to avoid having them "face" each other, but don't go to any special effort to make this happen. If they play on opposite teams, reduce their pitching role to "Backup" pitcher to fill in any of the other roles as needed. And, if you already have an even number of eight or more persons, let each ambidextrous person play as one player, either Lefty or Witey.

See Appendix B for more detailed information on ambidextrous players and Appendix C for information on pitching roles.

- **"Fielders"** – The pitcher is the only fielder during the game.
  - There is no running in this game unless the pitcher decides to get aggressive in fielding or the batter chooses to take the "homerun trot" after hitting a homerun, which I highly recommend. (The batter

---

[30] By the way, the author is such a person, as you probably have already guessed. Actually, it is not quite as hard as you might think, and it is good for the brain to be so challenged. So I recommend it to any brave soul who is willing to stick with it.

[31] The "none" role is considered a non-pitcher. Therefore, ambidextrous players should expect to pitch in any other role.

[32] Remember, Major League Baseball has rules that apply to ambidextrous players also.

should at least touch home plate after a homerun, but there is no need to force that.) The base runners are all "imaginary."[33]

Definitions

- **"At Bat" (AB)** – When the batter bats and the result is not a walk or hit by pitch. [34]

- **"Plate Appearance" (PA)** – When the batter bats regardless of the outcome.

- **"Batter Faced Pitcher" (BFP)** – When the pitcher pitches to the batter regardless of the outcome.

- **"Slot"** – A slot is a row on the scoresheet that shows a batter's activity during the game. Each slot has a number that is shown on the left-hand side.

- **"Time up" (to the plate)** – The time up to the plate includes all of what a batter does in the same inning and slot. It can include more than one "plate appearance" under certain situations. Examples for when this can happen are after a walk or after a hit by pitch. (For the second plate appearance, the batter hits off the tee.)

- **"Ground balls"** – These are batted balls that touch the ground in front of the yellow line.

- **"Fly balls"** – These are batted balls that touch or cross the yellow line on the fly.

The Game

- Even the game itself is "scaled" with respect to "9 innings."
  - The game lasts 9 innings configured as follows, with the 9th inning having 2 halves.[35]
  - Visitor's innings batting are 1, 3, 5, 7, "top of the 9th," and, if necessary, the "top of the 10th."
  - Home innings batting are 2, 4, 6, 8, "bottom of the 9th," and, if necessary, the "bottom of the 10th."

---

[33] Stand-in base runners – If you prefer (and they are willing), have youngsters stand in as base runners. This can be a good educational tool even though they act merely as human markers. (If they run too far, it is OK to put them back.)
[34] If you want to get fancy, you can score sacrifices as a non-at bat. We just never have done that.
[35] Normally configured, this would be 5 innings.

- If necessary, play a 10th inning tiebreaker (see tiebreaker rules). The tiebreaker can also result in an "11th inning" unearned run. No game lasts more than 11 "innings," and no batter ever bats in the 11th inning.

- Each inning (or half-inning for the 9th and 10th innings) has 4 batters come to the plate ("times up"), regardless of how many outs are recorded, as modified by the special rules for the tiebreaker inning. Stagger the leadoff batter for each inning according to the scoresheet.

- Each game uses one pitcher (for a "one-on-one" two-player game), two pitchers (for a "two-on-two" four-player game), or three pitchers per game each side (certain exceptions apply). Sometimes, 4 pitchers can be scheduled. The three basic pitching roles are: a starter, a relief pitcher, and the fireman (for extra innings). The starter pitches three innings during innings 1–6. After the 7th inning stretch, the relief pitcher pitches two innings during innings 7–9. The fireman pitches the extra innings 10 (and 11). In games with less than three pitchers available, the pitchers play multiple roles. For two pitchers, the relief pitcher doubles as the fireman.

- See the "Lineup Selection Worksheet" in Appendix C for the process to determine pitchers and lineups.

• **Nomenclature** – The nomenclature ("2–3") used in this book indicates the batter is safe at second base and any runners advance 3 bases, etc. Other examples are (X–1), the batter is out and all runners advance one base, or (1–X) the batter is safe at first and the lead runner is out, other runners advance one base. If a "B" is inserted, it indicates a base hit. For example, (2B–2) indicates a double with the runners advancing two bases and (1B–0) indicates a single, runners are forced, except that the runner on third base always scores on base hits. If a "W" is inserted, it indicates a walk. For example, (1W–2) indicates a one-base walk with the runners advancing two bases. And if an "E" is inserted, it indicates an error. For example, (1E–1) indicates a one-base error with the runners advancing one base.

• **The "Strike" and the "Ball"** – For years I wanted to be able to call balls and strikes without the aid of a human umpire. (It's not that I don't like umpires, it's just that everybody wanted to play.)[36] When I discovered the basket idea, my dream was realized. Place two standard size laundry baskets beside each other starting 1 foot behind home plate, each basket should face the pitcher horizontally. Raise the back end (long side) of the second basket about the height of a standard baseball, which can be accomplished by placing such

---

[36] I tried umpiring a softball game once. Wow! Did I gain a new respect for umpires!

balls (or 2 of the 9" plastic balls mentioned earlier) under the backside of the second basket.

If the pitcher throws a ball that lands in one of the baskets, or can,[37] it is a strike. To be considered "in the basket" (or can), the ball must either:

- Touch the bottom or hit two sides or edges of either basket or the back of the front board inclusive or
- Hit anywhere on the second strike zone board or
- Strike any object resting inside of either basket except the front of the front board or
- Hit the edge of the basket or front board, then bounce up (higher than the point of the edge).

A ball hitting the top of any one of the edges of the baskets, including the center edge and the front edge (or front board), without bouncing to a level higher than it hit, without going into a basket or striking a second edge, and without the batter swinging is a ball. In other words, whatever is not a strike is a ball.

Following are some other strike/ball considerations:

- The "Automatic Called Strike Three" – When a handicap board is straight up in the second basket, and the batter does not swing at a strike, he is automatically out on a called strike 3, regardless of the count before the pitch.
- The "Passed Ball" – A pitch at which the batter swings and misses, which pitch also misses the strike zone and the bat does not touch the board or the baskets, is called a "passed ball." For some handicaps, this pitch is a ball, not a strike.
- Batter Hits the Equipment – Sometimes the batter will swing and hit the basket or the board with the bat, and at the same time, the ball stops or moves forward passed the fifteen-foot (pink) line as extended. He does not actually have to hit the ball.[38] In this case, the batter can either accept the lie of the ball as a regular batted ball or accept a swing and a miss. If a fair ball stops behind the above line, it counts as a swing and a miss

---

37 When the can is used it becomes the strike zone. Place the bottom edge of a #10 can so that it is touching the back corner of home plate. Apply the same rules to the can as to the baskets. The pitcher may use the basket behind the can as a backboard. It is a good idea to cover the unused baskets to avoid confusion regarding what is the strike zone.
38 Indeed, it is sometimes difficult to tell whether the ball was hit or not.

automatically. (The pitcher is considered to have thrown a strike, as if the batter had reached out to touch the ball.) If the ball is foul, including in one of the baskets, treat it as a regular foul ball, using the foul ball rules.

- If the ball hits the batter anywhere during the swing and does not hit the bat, it is a miss and counts as a strike.

- If the ball hits both the bat and the batter in the hand, score as a regular batted ball.

- If the ball hits the bat, and then after leaving the bat, later hits the batter other than in the hand while the batter has at least one foot inside the batter's box inclusive, it is a foul ball. If both feet are outside the batter's box exclusive, the ball is dead at the point of contact with the batter, and the ball is played from there.

- If the batter, with a free hand, touches, bats, or catches the ball, it is scored as a swing and a miss. Otherwise, if the ball hits the batter without the batter swinging or crossing the front line of the batter's box toward home plate, it is a ball (and not a hit by pitch).[39]

- A pitched ball is dead when it touches the ground or an object such as the baskets, etc. If a batter begins his swing after a pitched ball is dead, it is not a swing.

- **The "Base Hit"**

    - Infield Single – Runners advance one base (1B–1), but, if allowed by the field plan (1B–1•, added dot), can convert to two bases (1B–2) for the last batter of the inning only. The pitcher throws from the front mound. (See the field plan [Default Lines in the preface] and the "Base-running Conversion" rule.) Do the conversion only if a run can score on the play (and it is the last batter of the inning).

    - Outfield Single – Runners advance two bases (1B–2), but, if allowed by the field plan (1B–2•), can convert to three bases (1B–3) for the last batter of the inning only. The pitcher throws from the front mound. (See the field plan [Default Lines in the preface] and the "Base-running Conversion" rule.)

    - Short Single – The runner on third scores, other runners are forced (1B–0). This situation applies only to fair balls hit to the pitcher or to the left

---

39   If the scorekeeper judges that the pitch would have been a ball anyway, and/or, if he deems best, he may issue a first-time warning on either infraction.

side of the infield inside the yellow line, as shown on the field plan. It does not apply to balls hit to the right side or passed the yellow line.

- Leftfield or rightfield double (passed the close Blue Line) - runners advance two bases (2B-2•), but can convert to three bases (2B-3) for the last batter of the inning only, as allowed by the "Base-running Conversion" rule. The pitcher throws from the back mound. (See the "Field Plan" and the "Base-running Conversion" rule.)
- Centerfield or left-centerfield double (passed the corner Blue Line) - clears the bases (2B-3)
- Triple - clears the bases (3B-3)
- Homeruns and other fencing activity[40]:
  - Automatic Triple – A fair-batted ball that bounces on the ground in front of and then over the homerun fence (barrier) in fair territory is a triple and the runners advance three bases (3B–3).
  - Automatic Double – A fair-batted ball that bounces on the ground in front of and then out of play over the homerun fence/line (black line extended) or other boundary line in foul territory is a double, and the runners advance three bases (2B–3).
  - Homerun – (The batter is encouraged to take the homerun "trot," but he should at least touch home plate. A pinch runner can be used, if desired.[41]):
    - The Black Line – The black line is the homerun line, fence, or barrier. A batted ball that hits any part of the fence or other type of obstruction[42] or barrier in fair territory without ever touching the ground in front of it, or behind it and bounces over or through the fence (at that point in either fair or foul territory) without ever touching the ground in play and lands on the ground or sits on an obstacle behind the fence is a homerun. If the homerun barrier is the side of a building (with a roof), score a homerun if it lands on the roof on the fly (bouncing up[43]), even if it eventually bounces

---

[40] Each ball field may have need for its own ground rules that may override these rules under special circumstances.
[41] Hey! This game is all about having fun. So don't be bashful. Celebrate! (By the way, in our league everyone on both teams congratulates each other for hitting homeruns.)
[42] Including the pitcher. See the section on obstructions in chapter 3 for specific rules.
[43] If it bounces down, it probably hit the side of the building. In that case, score the ball as still in play (where it lies).

or rolls back onto the playing field. Additionally, a paved road (not dirt or gravel) can count as a "barrier," in which case, score a homerun if the batted ball hits the pavement on the fly.[44] If there is no type of barrier, score the same as "other colored lines" (below).

- It is a very good idea to have some sort of homerun barrier that will allow you to see whether the batted ball crosses the homerun line on the fly. If you have no such barrier, I recommend adding 15 literal feet of distance to the black line and score a homerun when the ball bounces or rolls across this new black line. Also, extend the orange line to replace the vacated default black line, which extends the inside-the-park homerun area.

  o Other Colored Lines (no fences, inside the playing field) – For certain handicaps, the ball merely needs to touch or cross the line on the fly or the bounce.

- Other Hits

  o A fair-batted ball that hits the fence (barrier) in fair or foul territory and stays on the ground in play is a fair ball and is scored as it lies.

  o Score a batted ball that is stuck in, or remains on, the fence as if it is part of the fence on the ground at the inside base of the fence (playing field side) straight down.

- Batter's Box and Batter's Circle

  o The catcher (if you use one) is the only person, other than the batter, that is allowed inside the batter's circle during play. His only activity is to retrieve balls. Play must halt until the batter's circle is clear of everyone except the batter and the catcher.

  o If the batter, while standing or striding during the pitch, places any part of either foot across the line closest to home plate, he is out of the batter's box. All such pitches are strikes, whether they are in the strike zone or not, regardless of whether the batter swings. (He can cross the other three lines as long as he has one foot in the box inclusive.)

  o If, during the pitch, the batter takes his batting position (or strides) with all of both feet outside of the batter's box inclusive, treat the batter as "trying for a tee shot." See the "Batting From the Tee" and "Try for a Tee

---

[44] You will hear a smack and/or see a bounce.

Shot" rules (below). In order for this rule to apply, the batter must admit to being ready to receive the pitch and/or be "informed of his rights."[45]

- **Fair Ball/Foul Ball**[46] (for foul outs, see "Base Runners" below):
  - The Bases
    - If the batted ball touches the base (the white flag), the ball is fair. However, if the white flag is not covering its marker, play the ball as it lies.
    - If the batted ball stops before the base, the ball is fair or foul based on the lie of the ball.[47]
    - If the batted ball stops after the base:
      - If the ball touches ground fair just before it passes the base and also just after it passes the base, it is fair regardless of where it stops.
      - If the ball touches ground foul just before it passes the base and also just after it passes the base, it is fair if it stops in fair territory and foul if it stops in foul territory.[48]
      - If the ball touches ground fair just before it passes the base and foul just after it passes the base, it is fair regardless of where it stops.
      - If the ball touches ground foul just before it passes the base and fair just after it passes the base, it is fair regardless of where it stops.
      - If the ball is fair when it lands after the base, it is fair regardless of where it stops.

---

45 The batter can change his mind during all this; it is the last pitch that makes the final determination, and then, only if it is a ball or a hit by pitch.
46 The foul lines themselves are considered to be in fair territory.
47 It is good to mark important points on your field with corresponding colored flags lying on the ground. If the batted ball touches any of the colored flags (not white), play the ball as it lies.
48 If a foul-batted ball contacts the foul barrier, the ball is considered either fair or foul "after it passes the base" regardless what happens to the ball after hitting the barrier. In other words, the foul barrier cannot make a foul ball fair and vice versa.

- If the ball is foul when it lands after the base, it is fair if it stops in fair territory and foul if it stops in foul territory.[49]
- The Foul Pole[50]
  - If the batted ball touches the foul pole, the ball is fair.
  - If the ball is fair when it passes the pole, it is fair regardless of where it lands or stops.
  - If the ball is foul when it passes the pole, it is fair if it lands or stops in fair territory, otherwise, it is foul.
  - If the ball is fair when it lands, it is fair regardless of where it stops.
  - If the ball is foul when it lands, it is fair if it stops in fair territory.
- In cases when a fair ball stops in foul territory, extend all applicable lines into foul territory to determine the outcome of the play. See the field plan for the positions of the line extensions. The foul barrier/boundary is the extension of the homerun line. If there is no foul barrier/boundary, the homerun line "extends" into foul territory perpendicular to the foul line.

- **The "Balk"**
  - If, while the batter is ready and waiting, the pitcher pumps either hand more than one time without throwing the ball, it is a balk.
  - A warning shall be given to each pitcher on the first infraction in any given game.
  - On a balk, all runners advance one base and a ball is credited to the batter. (If this is ball four, apply the extra base after applying the results of the walk.)

- **Batting From the Tee**
  - When the batter bats from the tee:
    - The pitcher becomes a spectator and takes a position on the sidelines out of play.

---

49   If a foul-batted ball contacts the foul barrier, the ball is considered either fair or foul "after it passes the base" regardless what happens to the ball after hitting the barrier. In other words, the foul barrier cannot make a foul ball fair and vice versa.
50   If there is no foul pole, or the test is inconclusive, ignore this rule.

- The tee is placed anywhere behind home plate between the batters' boxes exclusive and extended.
- The batter does not have to stand in either of the batter's boxes.
- Suspend the hit by pitch rule. Balls hit into the basket(s) are foul balls.
- The batter cannot bunt.
- The batter may take as many swings at the ball as he had strikes left when ball four was thrown until he hits a fair ball, strikes out, or fouls out (on a two-strike count).
  - Count foul balls as strikes. If he hits a foul ball with 2 strikes, play all the normal foul out rules.
  - If the batter hits the tee and the ball falls off the tee without the bat hitting the ball, score a strike.
  - If the batter strikes out, score a multiple play using the foul out rules ("strike 'em out, throw 'em out").
  - Do not count as a swing when the batter hits nothing at all, even if the ball falls off the tee.
- On a fair ball or foul out, play the ball as it lies, according to the various handicaps and other applicable rules.
  - As an alternative to using the tee, the batter may choose to "pitch to himself" by tossing the ball and trying to hit it in the air. Change the tee rules as follows; all other rules stay the same:
    - "Improper Stance" – Both feet must start and alight within either of the batter's boxes inclusive through, and just after, contact of the bat with the ball.
    - Score a swing and a miss, or an "improper stance," as a strike.
  - The "WILDcard" Tee – If the "walk chart" indicates a "WILDcard" tee, the batter is allowed to choose any bat (including the fat orange bat) and any ball (including the 9" and 12" plastic balls) for his tee shot.
- **"Try for a Tee Shot"** – The batter may choose at any time during his time up to bat to "try for a tee shot." (This is automatic if the batter is absent, unless a substitute can be found. See below.)

- If he is present, the batter places the tee in a batter's box (optional) and then remains present[51] while the pitcher pitches to the empty batter's box. If he places the tee, he is not actually an "absent" batter and, therefore, if he walks, he draws his walk from the regular walk chart, as normally called for in the walk rules. (If the tee is not placed, or he does not bat after the walk, he is treated as absent, and his walk is scored from "absent batter" on the walk chart.) Either way, he accepts a walk or a strikeout as the pitching outcome dictates. If he draws a walk, he can then bat again using the tee (following regular walk rules). If he is not present or elects not to hit off the tee, his time up to bat is over.
- If the batter is nowhere in sight, he bats according to the "Absent Batter" rules (see chapter 5). If his presence is detected before the first pitch to the next batter, let him restart his time up from the beginning or, if he already walked as an absent batter,[52] he can hit off the tee.

- **The "Walk"**
  - Generally, depending on the pitcher's handicap, a walk is four balls pitched in a row without scoring a strike or batted ball.[53] For any strike or foul ball that is not an out, the ball count restarts at zero. However, some pitcher's handicaps count the balls differently. For example, there are times when regular baseball count rules apply.
  - Either 1-base, 2-base, or 3-base walks can be scored.
  - Sometimes a walk will allow runners to advance more bases than the batter does.
  - See the "walk chart" on the scoresheet for the disposition of walks in different situations. If "WILD" or "XB" is indicated, the batter bats off the tee (limited to two plate appearances total in one time up). If "WILD" is indicated, also follow the rules for the "WILD" card tee in the "Batting From the Tee" rules (above).
  - "Weak Pitcher" – (Ignore this rule while you are pitching to Dead Ringer or when either the batter or the pitcher is absent.)
    - If a pitcher gives up at least two of any combination of 2-base or 3-base walks in any inning, he is "weak." (1-base walks do not count.) For the rest of his scheduled stint, he is subject to replacement by

---

51 Yes, he or she may sit in the shade.
52 Still score his walk from "absent batter" on the walk chart.
53 The pitcher may orally call for an intentional walk. Count as many thrown balls as needed to score the walk, then follow normal walk rules. The batter may then hit off the tee.

the next pitcher in line, who then would continue into his regular stint. He may be replaced at the scorekeeper's discretion, depending on the pitcher's attitude.[54] Everything being satisfactory, I suggest replacing him if the third batter is coming up. At this point he still has two batters left—half of the inning—having pitched only walks (that count) in the inning so far. If there is only the fourth batter left to bat, let him finish the inning and then bring in the next pitcher at the start of the next inning.

- If the weak pitcher is the fireman (or no one is scheduled to pitch after him), then he continues to pitch as normal, unless a bona fide substitute is found. Any pitcher on his team who is not scheduled to pitch that day may substitute for him. However, if no substitute can be found, the scorekeeper has the option to have him pitch absentee for the rest of his stint.

- Whenever a pitcher throws two 3-base walks in the same inning, or he displays a bad attitude, consider whether his role should be changed to "specialist" or "none" for the future, or, in extreme cases, whether he should even remain on the team. Hopefully, the extreme situations can be avoided.

- **Base Runners, Outs, and Foul Outs**

    o If the fourth batter of the inning is out, the inning is over and no runners advance. (This means that the objective of the fourth batter is to drive the ball.)

    o Fair-batted ground balls (or "fly balls" inside the yellow line that are not caught) that are outs, regardless of how many outs there are or how many batters have batted, play as follows: to the right of second base, all runners advance one base (X–1). To the left of second base or in front of the pitcher (areas 99, 301, 302), the runner on second base is forced; all other runners advance one base. Except for the fourth batter of the inning, the runner on third base always scores.

    o With certain exceptions, all foul balls are outs and scored as a foul out to the catcher, runners hold (X–0). The exceptions are as follows:

        - Foul balls that pass the homerun line extended[55] (and thus out of play) are not outs. The batter may continue to bat. Score a strike, but

---

54   If the pitcher displays a bad attitude, you may choose to replace him at any time, bringing in the next slated pitcher.
55   See the section on "fair ball/foul ball" above.

not a strikeout or foul out. (The only exception is for quadruple play situations, in which case, all foul balls are outs.[56])

- Foul balls that pass the foul territory barrier (if used)—if there is a barrier or boundary line in foul territory and the foul ball passes over that barrier line, except for quadruple play situations—consider the batted ball to be out of play. Score as a strike, but not a strikeout or a foul out.

- Foul balls that pass the extra base hit line extended[57] (and still in play), except for quadruple play situations, foul balls, are single outs only (not multiple outs), and are scored as a foul out to the outfielder, and runners advance one base (X–1).

- See "The 'Double Play' and More" below for more detailed information.

- If either the pitchers or the batters are dominating the league, the foul out rules may be adjusted and/or relaxed. Any such modifications will be indicated on, or through, the lineup selection worksheet or through the scorekeeper's records. (See Appendix C.)

- **The "Bunt"**

    o The batter has the option to bunt. He announces his intention to bunt if he "squares around"[58] but does not have to square around if he announces it orally.[59] He then can advance base runners one base with a fair ball out (just as normal) if the batted ball stays inside the white line and he keeps the ball away from the pitcher and the catcher (for specifics, see "area criteria" below).

    - Ignore other base hit or homerun lines.

    - He may use the fat orange bat. Otherwise, unauthorized use of the fat orange bat will be assumed to be an announced bunt attempt.

    - He cannot bunt off the tee.

    - Batted balls that stop in a basket (or the can) are foul balls, not a hit-by-pitch.

---

56   Ignore the foul territory barriers or boundaries during quadruple play situations only.
57   See the field plan for the extensions of the colored lines.
58   Or holds the bat straight out, or stops his swing in the straight out position.
59   He can choose to swing at the ball anyway, if he wants to. However, all rules are the same; he still has to keep the ball inside the white line to be successful.

- The last batter of the inning cannot advance any runners on a bunt unless he gets a base hit.
  - "Area Criteria" (see the field plan [Default Lines in the preface])
    - If the ball comes to rest within area 403 on the field plan, it is a single (1B–1).
    - If the ball comes to rest in area 99, 103, or 503, the lead runner is out, other runners advance 1 base and the batter is on first base on a fielder's choice.
    - If the ball comes to rest in areas 302, 303, or 304, it is a double play (only) with the batter and the lead runner being called out. Other runners advance one base.
    - If the batted ball passes the white line, it is a quadruple play possibility (see below).
    - Any foul ball is a quadruple play possibility (see below).
    - For all other areas, the batter is out and the runners advance one base (X–1).
- **Dead Ball**
  - A batted ball is dead when the motion of the ball has stopped or the pitcher traps the ball between his body and the ground (thus stopping the ball). In the case of a trap, the ball is considered "in play" at the location of the trap and the play ruled from that spot.
  - A pitched ball is dead when it touches the ground or an object, such as the baskets, the batter, or the catcher, etc. If a batter begins his swing after a pitched ball is dead, it is not a swing.
- **The "Double Play" and More**
  - If the pitcher catches a batted ball on the fly (not a homerun or otherwise out of play[60]) anywhere in either fair or foul territory, the batter is out regardless of what the batter's handicap is. If there is at least one runner

---

60   If a fair ball, when a catch is secured and the fielder's motion has stopped or the farthest advance of the ball, one foot is, or at any time during contact with the ball, was at least on or behind the batter's homerun line, the batted ball is a homerun. If a foul ball, when a catch is secured and the fielder's motion has stopped or the farthest advance of the ball one foot is, or at any time during contact with the ball, was at least on or behind the foul ball barrier, the batted ball is "out of play" and not a catch. If on, or straddling, the foul line at the time of the catch, it is fair at that point.

on base, it is a multiple play. See double, triple, and quadruple outs below. Runners hold. (In other words, treat any fly ball caught by the pitcher that is in play as if it were a foul ball inside, or before it reaches, the batter's base hit area.)

- A batted ground ball (not otherwise a base hit[61]) that is caught or stops within the double play area (this is everything fair inside the yellow base hit line exclusive) is a double play ground ball. If there is a runner on first base, it is a double play (only).

- "Double Foul out" and "Double Play" – A foul out (in play, whether or not the ball is caught by the pitcher) or a fly ball caught in play in a double foul out scenario is a double play possibility. The lead runner is out and other runners hold. Extra base hit and foul barrier rules apply.

- "Triple Foul out" and "Triple Play" – A foul out (in play, whether or not the ball is caught by the pitcher) or a fly ball caught in play in a triple foul out scenario is a triple play possibility. The two lead runners are out and the other runner holds. Extra base hit and foul barrier rules apply.

- "Quadruple Foul out" and "Quadruple Play" – This play is done differently than the others. A foul ball (whether or not the ball is caught by the pitcher) or a fly ball caught in play in a quadruple foul out scenario is a quadruple play possibility, which (should it actually come to fruition) is a rare event, because all three of the first batters have to have reached base without scoring, and the fourth batter is the last batter of the inning. Therefore, we make the following exception. All foul balls result in the batter and all current base runners being out. Ignore foul boundaries and extra base hit areas. All the base runners are out. This situation arises always and only when the pitcher's handicap is "plaid," or when a bunt is exercised.

- Base Runners in a Double or Triple Play[62]

    - If caught on the fly, fair or foul, the batter and the lead runner(s) are out, starting with the runner on third base, etc. All other runners hold.

    - If a foul ball is not caught, all runners who are not out hold their positions. However, do not score more than one out on foul balls that are not caught when they have passed the extended extra base hit line. In this case, the runner on third base scores, other runners hold.

---

61   If, when the catch is secured and the fielder's motion has stopped or the farthest advance of the ball, one foot is, or at any time during contact with the ball was, at least on or behind the batter's base hit line, the batted ball is a base hit.
62   This would not apply to quadruple play situations.

(Remember, except for the quadruple foul out scenario, foul balls that are passed the foul boundaries are not foul outs.)

- If it is a fair ground ball, the batter and the runner on first base are out and it is a double play only. This only applies when there is a runner on first base. (Other runners advance one base.)

- **The "Hit By Pitch"** – A batted ball that comes to rest in either basket or can, either on the fly or on the bounce, is ruled a hit by pitch (HBP or HP). The batter advances to first base and any runners are forced (1–0). The batter is allowed to bat again one time during the same inning using a regular tee, but he cannot bat more than twice in the same inning. (A runner on third base scores only if the bases are loaded.)

- **The "Stolen Base"** – Please note: Dead Ringer, either as a pitcher or as a runner, is listed separately below for each throwing chance. Absent pitchers and runners follow Dead Ringer's rules unless they are present and they choose to participate in steal situations. Such can be the case if the pitcher carries the "none" role or a batter remains present after his time up is over. (See Appendix C for information on pitching roles.)

  o Before the first pitch is thrown to a new batter, either the captain[63], the runner with an open base in front of him, or the batter can call for an attempt at a good lead. (However, the runner has the final say in whether he actually makes a throw.) The pitcher then tries to throw a strike without the batter or any strike zone boards present. If successful, there is not a good lead and no base stealing can take place. Once the last batter of the inning is finished batting, no one can try for a good lead.[64]

  o **Straight Steal of Second or Third**[65]

    - =1= If the pitcher throws from second base

      o STRIKE, stealer is out, others hold

      o BALL, stealer throws from close (the close mound) [go to =3=]

      o No throw, pitcher throws from the back mound [go to =2=]

      o Dead Ringer pitching, stealer throws from the close mound [go to =3=]

---

63 The scorekeeper can recognize a captain for each team for this purpose.
64 Yes, this question has come up.
65 If there are runners on first and third, the runner on third holds. See the "delayed double steal" and the "straight steal of home" below if you want to try to steal using a runner on third.

- **=2=** If the stealer is on first base, pitcher throws from back. If the stealer is on 2nd base, pitcher throws from close
  - STRIKE, all runners hold
  - BALL, stealer throws from close [go to =3=]
  - No throw, stealer is safe, others hold
  - Dead Ringer pitching, stealer throws from the close mound [go to =3=]
- **=3=** Stealer throws from the close mound
  - STRIKE, safe, others advance
  - BALL, out, others advance
  - No throw, out on pickoff, others hold
  - Dead Ringer stealing, out, others advance

- **Delayed Double Steal** (only with runners on 1st and 3rd)
  - **=4=** If the pitcher throws from second base
    - STRIKE, first is out, third holds
    - BALL, first throws from close [go to =6=]
    - No throw, pitcher throws from back [go to =5=]
    - Dead Ringer pitching, third throws from close, first is safe at second [go to =8=]
  - **=5=** If the pitcher throws from back
    - STRIKE, runners hold (the play is off)
    - BALL, first throws from close [go to =6=]
    - No throw, first is safe at second base, third holds
    - Dead Ringer pitching, third throws from close, first is safe at second [go to =8=]
  - **=6=** Runner on first throws from close (good lead from a ball)
    - STRIKE, first is safe at second, pitcher throws from back [go to =7=]

- BALL, first is tentative,[66] pitcher throws from close [go to =7=]
- No throw, play the hit and run (optional)
- Dead Ringer stealing, first is tentative, pitcher throws from close [go to =7=]

- **=7=** Pitcher throws from close or back
  - STRIKE, third throws from back, first is safe at second [go to =9=]
  - BALL, third throws from close, first is safe at second [go to =8=]
  - No throw, third is safe at home; if the runner on first is tentative, he is out at second
  - Dead Ringer pitching, third throws from close, first is safe at second [go to =8=]

- **=8=** Runner on third throws from close mound
  - STRIKE, safe at home, others hold
  - BALL, out at home, others hold
  - No throw, out at home, others hold
  - Dead Ringer stealing, out at home, others hold

- **=9=** Runner on third throws from back mound
  - STRIKE, safe at home, others hold
  - BALL, out at home, others hold
  - No throw, runners hold (second and third)
  - Dead Ringer stealing, out at home, others hold

  o **Straight Steal of Home** (first base must be empty; the hit and run play is not available)

  - **=10=** If the pitcher throws from second base
    - STRIKE, stealer is out, others hold
    - BALL, stealer throws from back [go to =12=]
    - No throw, pitcher throws from close [go to =11=]
    - Dead Ringer pitching, stealer throws from back [go to =12=]

---

[66] The outcome will be determined later in the play.

- =11= If the pitcher throws from close (or back)
    - STRIKE, all runners hold
    - BALL, stealer throws from back [go to =12=]
    - No throw, stealer is safe at home, others hold
    - Dead Ringer pitching, stealer throws from back [go to =12=]
- =12= Stealer throws from back mound
    - STRIKE, safe, others advance
    - BALL, out, others advance
    - No throw, out on pickoff, others hold
    - Dead Ringer stealing, out, others advance
- **The "Hit and Run" Play (2nd or 3rd base must be open)**[67]
    - After obtaining a good lead (either 1st or 2nd base), instead of stealing immediately, the captain or the batter may decide to invoke the hit-and-run play. The runner(s) attempt(s) to steal only if the batter strikes out. (The runner has no say in this, but he can decline to throw the ball, which, if happens, is scored as "caught stealing.")[68]
    - If the batter hits the ball, make the following adjustments:
        - No Double Play on a Ground Ball – A ground out[69] is a ground out 1-base advance for the runners (X–1).
        - Black-X – The batter may choose the "Black-X" handicap, regular bat, regular balls, no strike zone boards; or he may choose to keep his stated handicap, or the pitcher's handicap, if available.
        - Extra Base – If a base hit results, base runners advance an extra base. In addition, if the runner wants to score from first base on a single-two-base advance (1B–2) he may attempt that through conversion. The pitcher throws from the close mound. (See the "Base-running Conversion" rule below.)
        - All other plays are the same.

---

[67] The runner on third is irrelevant to the hit and run.
[68] Dead Ringer is an automatic caught stealing.
[69] See the definition of a ground ball (above).

- **The Base-running Conversion** – When the rules allow, the runner may try to take an extra base. If so, the pitcher may choose to try to throw a strike either from second base or from the regular pitcher's plate ("mound") or, sometimes, as called for, from the close pitcher's plate. If the pitcher is successful from either pitcher's plate, the target runner is safe at the original base (that is, he cannot advance the extra base). If the pitcher is successful from second base, the runner is out at the target base. In all cases, trailing runners advance one base unless the pitcher elects to hold the ball and not throw. Note: Dead Ringer's throws are never successful, so his strategy should be to hold the ball.

- **The "Inside the Park" Homerun** – When a batted ball comes to rest within the inside the park homerun area (orange line; IP-HR, IpHR), an inside the park homerun possibility exists for black, orange, or turquoise power handicaps.[70] Score originally as a triple. At the batter's option, he can convert the triple into a homerun. (See the "Base-running Conversion" rule above.)

- **The Pitcher and the Batter Are the Same Person**

    - If the pitcher and the batter are both the same live person, for the first time up, bat off the tee using the "absent pitcher" rules, except do not allow for walks. *Do not steal or play the hit and run.* For every subsequent time up for this player, look at the previous time up.[71] If he made an out, he bats off the tee, as above. If he got on base (or hit a homerun), pitch to him absentee and follow the "absent batter" rules.

    - If the pitcher and the batter are both absent, Dead Ringer or otherwise, follow the rules outlined in the section titled "If Dead Ringer Pitches to Himself" in chapter 5.

- **The "Tiebreaker"** – If the game is tied after the normal number of innings, play a 10th tiebreaker inning. Each team bats up to one full round, similar to the other innings. First, the visiting team bats until there are four batters.[72] Then the home team bats until they have more runs than the visitors or they bat all four batters, whichever comes first, after which the results are calculated. This ends the inning.

    - After both teams have had a chance to bat, the winner is the team that has:

        - The most runs scored. If this is a tie, then …

---

70 For all other handicaps, it would already be a homerun.
71 Whether in this slot or another slot, the slot is irrelevant. Go with his last time up.
72 Five batters for regulation baseball.

- The earliest "time up (slot)" in which a run is scored (based on who batted him in). If this is a tie, then …
- Most base running points.[73] If this is a tie, then …
- Fewest total out points (as listed below). Only count the batter's end of a multiple play:
    - 1 point for outs of any kind to the warning track[74]
    - 2 points for outs of any kind to outfielders[75]
    - 3 points for outs of any kind to infielders[76]
    - 4 points for ground outs to the pitcher[77]
    - 5 points for pop or fly outs to the pitcher (caught on the fly)
    - 6 points for outs of any kind to the catcher[78]
    - 7 points for strikeouts
- If the out points are tied, the visiting team is the winner

o Apply the same substitution rules as are used earlier in the game.

o Award enough runs ("unearned") to the winner of the tiebreaker inning over the actual score to secure the lead (generally, just one). If there are any unearned runs, score them as an 11th inning.

---

73   Add the values for each runner on base: 1st=1, 2nd =2, 3rd=4.
74   In miniature baseball, the "warning track" is the extra base hit area that allows a three-base advance according to the batter's handicap. Generally, this would be the center, left-center, or right-center field areas. (For the blue line, this would mean the areas passed the corner blue lines.)
75   Passed the yellow line on the fly. (For baseball, this would include outfielders throwing out base runners).
76   First base, second base, third base, or shortstop; not pitchers or catchers. The ball must bounce in front of and pass over the yellow line.
77   Ground outs are any outs that touch the ground in front of the yellow line which may, or may not, pass over the yellow line. The pitcher's area is that area between the 15-foot (pink) line inclusive and the yellow line exclusive. The ball must stop within this area to be the pitcher's play.
78   The catcher's area is between the 15-foot (pink) line exclusive and home plate.

Chapter 3

"Fundamentals"—Technical Issues

Application of the Rules

- Any rules can be changed for the whole game before the start of the game by unanimous consent or for certain situations during the game by either unanimous consent or unanimous default.[79] Throwing the first pitch to the next batter closes the door on unanimous default unless changed for specific situations by unanimous consent. The scorekeeper acts as an arbitrator in all this and has the final say. In other situations, if a mistake is made in applying the rules, except for batting out of turn, all play after the first errant play inclusive, up to, but not including, the first pitch to the next batter after the errant play can be replayed at the scorekeeper's discretion. By default, once the first pitch to the next batter is thrown, prior activity is not replayed. But again, the scorekeeper can override all this and has the final say.

- Batting out of turn

    - If a batter bats early (out of turn), do not automatically call him out or negate his play. Rather, if the batter gets on base or hits a homerun, let

---

[79] For example, if nobody says anything.

him decide whether to replay or to hold his play (to be applied to his turn at the plate in the proper order). If there is an out, let the pitcher decide. This decision can be made at the proper time to bat. If the errant time up is carried forward (i.e., not replayed at the proper time to replay it), do not allow any base stealing.

- o If a mistake is discovered before the completion of an at bat, restart the count for his time up at the proper time. If discovered while hitting off the tee, finish the tee shot and suspend the whole time up until the proper time.

- Rule conflicts go to the pitcher. Even though I have tried to eliminate rule conflicts, the possibility does exist. This would involve conflicts between different written rules. Unless the rule states otherwise, the pitcher chooses which rule will be applied. (Exception: the scorekeeper will decide regarding the interpretation of individual rules.)

- Field conflicts go the batter. When a conflict arises involving activity relating to action on the field, a notable example being when the ball is straddling a line (and the rules are not a factor), unless the rule states otherwise, the batter makes the choice. When allowed in the rules, the batter can also use the options outlined in Appendix E. (Exception: the scorekeeper will decide regarding trees and bushes as obstructions. See below.)

Scoring – The Flavor of the Game

- I believe baseball scoring should reflect the nature of the game. It does not need to look like basketball (125–116) or football (31–24). Even softball scores can be too high (14–8). When you have baseball scores this high, the nature of the game becomes offensive in the sense that the power aspect of offence is emphasized to the minimization of finesse. The sacrifice, the stolen base, advancing the runners, avoiding the double play, etc., take a back seat in the nature of the game when you are constantly hoping for the grand slam homerun. On the other hand, it doesn't need to constantly look like soccer, either (2–1 or 1–1).[80] Yes, baseball games with low scores are indeed exciting in their own right because the little things are enlarged, but too many low scoring games can get boring in the long run. Therefore, I recommend that miniature baseball scoring should average between 7 and 8 runs per game, total both sides. This will give you a good sprinkling of scores that range

---

[80] Probably the sport that comes closest to what baseball scoring should look like is hockey (3–2).

between 1–0 and 7–6 (or higher), the latter score I have found to be rather invigorating.[81] So here are some recommendations:

- Keep track of your league's average runs per game (total both sides). This will tell you if your hitters or pitchers are dominating the league.
    - If, after at least five games, and after each game thereafter, your average is 8.5 to 9.49 runs per game or more, add an out to the foul ball situation. In other words, a foul out can result in a double play with the lead runner.
    - If your average is 9.5 runs per game or more, add two outs to the foul ball situation. In other words, a foul out can result in a triple play with the lead runners.
    - On the other hand, if your pitchers are dominating the league, resulting in your average runs being less than 4.5 per game, subtract an out from the foul ball situation. In other words, a foul ball will not result in a foul out.
    - You should also adjust the "handicap conversion chart" on the "lineup selection worksheet," based on average runs per game. Use the following chart to make your adjustments. See the "lineup selection worksheet" in Appendix C.
        - 0 to 3.49 runs/game = -20
        - 3.5 to 4.49 runs/game = -10
        - 4.5 to 6.49 runs/game = -5
        - 6.5 to 8.49 runs/game = 0
        - 8.5 to 9.49 runs/game = +5
        - 9.5 to 10.49 runs/game = +10
        - >= 10.5 runs/game = +20
    - Besides runs per game, it is not good to allow the homeruns to languish either, for this is an exciting aspect of the game. Too little, or (believe it or not) too many, can cause the game to become boring in the long haul. This situation is most likely to become an issue if you have a league that is skewed toward the younger players. It is best to get the whole family involved. To monitor this situation, you should keep track of your league's average homeruns per game, also:

---

[81] For me personally, scores higher than 7–6 become a little melodramatic and overstimulating, lacking finesse.

- After at least five games, and after each game thereafter, if your league's average homeruns per game (for both sides) is less than 1.0, the "quick and dirty" option is to change the actual colors of the lines on the field. (Make the blue line black[82], make the red line blue, make the grey line red, make the yellow line grey, make the white line yellow, and consider the purple and the white lines the same.) However, the preferred option is to change the power colors (only) on the batters handicap markers. This can be done by making new markers or by using overlays.

- If your league's average homeruns per game (for both sides) is greater than or equal to 2.5 but less than 3.0, use the orange ball for everyone with a black power handicap or below and the turquoise ball for orange and turquoise handicaps.

- If your league's average homeruns per game (for both sides) is greater than or equal to 3.0, use the turquoise ball for everyone.

Field Design

- Examples of field plans appear in the preface, illustrating the principles we have just discussed. First is the standard field plan showing the default lines. Second is the same basic plan with a modified black line superimposed.

- There are three types of lines: default, standard, and adjustable.

    o **Default Lines** – When setting up a ball field, the first thing you want to do, as far as possible, is to mark on your field where all the default field lines will go. The default positions of these lines are found on the Default Field Plan, the first of the field plans in the preface. See Appendix D for instructions on how to stake the default lines.

    o **Standard Lines** – These are all the lines from home plate to the "closer blue lines." All the standard lines are firmly set intact and should not be adjusted.[83]

    o **Adjustable Lines** – The "corner blue lines,"[84] orange line, and black line (the "fence") are not part of the standard set of lines. The black line can be moved. The orange and the corner blue lines can be truncated or extended as the situation dictates.

---

82   Do this by putting black markers where the blue line would ordinarily be, etc.
83   This does not mean they cannot be adjusted, but that such adjustments are discouraged.
84   Those going to the left field and right field corners, that is, the farther distance blue lines.

- After the default lines are set, then set the black line. That line can fluctuate based on the lay of the land, the particular baseball field you want to model, your own personal preference, or whether you even use a homerun barrier. For best results, the black line should not be closer than any part of the standard blue line, that is, the closer distance blue lines. If any of the black line encroaches in the standard blue area, you should consider modifying the black line.[85]

- Then set the corner blue lines, that is, the farther distance blue lines, as adjusted above. If your custom black line is less than 350 scale feet (140 literal feet) down the lines, superimpose the black line over these blue lines. A blue mark should be indicated at the spot where the corner blue line intersects the black line or the foul line, whichever applies.

- The same is true for the orange lines. These lines can be truncated or extended. Superimpose the custom black line over the orange lines for the standard field. An orange mark should be indicated at the spots where the orange lines intersect the black line. (If the black line is set close enough, the orange line might be deleted altogether.) In addition, any area still inside the superimposed black line that exceeds the default black line is considered the orange area. These should be marked also.[86] (See the center field and right field areas on the field plan [Default Lines in the preface] for illustrations.)

- It is best to keep your field completely free of any obstructions, especially trees and bushes—not only on the ground but also in the air. Move or cut them away, if necessary. Especially, do not place your field, or allow on your field, a situation that causes any part of any bush or tree trunk to be in fair territory on, or inside, the yellow line. However, never move your spouse's favorite gazebo …[87]

Technical Conflicts

- Most field conflicts go to the batter. The batter makes the choice. However, regarding trees and bushes, the scorekeeper should make that decision. Before the game starts, it is best that everyone understand the specific application of each tree and bush that may affect any play in fair territory.

---

85   Otherwise, if you must, truncate the standard blue line.
86   Placing the orange lines is indicated whether or not you use a homerun barrier, because if you are not using a barrier, you need to extend the black line by 15 literal feet anyway. This extra space would be the orange area
87   … without permission, of course. Your life will be happier that way. But do try to align your field so that the gazebo is outside the yellow line.

- Obstructions (if a batted ball hits an obstruction)
  - **Real Estate** – This includes buildings, structures, logs and rocks (other than sticks and stones[88]), other heavy items on (or attached to) the ground, and any items declared by the owner of the field to be permanent.[89] (This section does not include balls, grass, sticks and stones, leaves, trees, players and clothing, spectators, animals, wires, or the homerun barrier. For these others, see below.)
    - Score the play from where the ball stops.
    - If the obstruction is in fair territory, the ball is fair regardless of where it stops. If the obstruction is in foul territory and the batted ball is not otherwise fair (such as passing over a base, etc.), the ball is foul regardless of where it stops. Score foul balls from where the ball stops for outs and base running purposes.
    - Except for homerun and foul boundary barriers, if the obstruction straddles the foul line, the ball is fair or foul depending on where it stops. However, if the ball hits a base that is properly situated, it is a fair ball, so make sure the bases are always properly situated on top of their respective ground markers.[90]
    - If a batted ball touches an obstruction other than any flags that might be within the batter's circle, or if the ball contacts the catcher within the batter's circle, the ball is dead at that point.
  - **Balls**
    - A ball hitting another ball in the field is rare, but it can happen. To reduce confusion, encourage the players to keep the field inside the yellow line free of loose balls. However, don't make a big deal out of it, for these rules will be their own encouragement if an issue truly arises. If you keep the field completely free of balls, you have no issue, but I'll leave it to you to decide whether this is practical for you.
    - For fair balls:[91]

---

88   The difference between "sticks and stones" and "logs and rocks" is that sticks and stones can be picked up and moved easily by one person.
89   Such as swings, gazebos, and campfire pits, etc.
90   For first and third bases, approximately half of the base should actually be in foul territory, but the batted ball that hits any part of the base is a fair ball.
91   Besides the other fair ball rules, if a batted ball touches any ball in fair territory, the batted ball is a fair ball, regardless of where it stops.

- If the obstruction is the stash of balls for the pitcher (well defined[92]), play as it lies.

- If the obstruction is any ball not within the stash of balls for the pitcher, all affected balls are in play. The batter decides which ball will determine the outcome of the play. If not already a homerun, the batter has some options:

    o If any affected ball is inside the turquoise line (exclusive), he may choose the lie of any affected ball.

    o If all affected balls are passed the turquoise line (inclusive) and at least one is inside the yellow line (exclusive), he may use the options outlined in Appendix E.

    o If all affected balls are passed the yellow line (inclusive), he may choose the lie of any affected ball.

  o If a foul-batted ball hits another ball (in foul territory), it is ruled a foul ball regardless of the outcome of either ball.

- **Grass** – Play as the ball lies. If the ball is stuck in grass above the surface of the ground, score the play as if the ball were lying on the ground straight down directly below.[93]

    o You need to pay attention to the grass; it is very important. (Remember, you are playing with "golf-ball" sized baseballs.) The length of the grass can vary depending on the type of game you want to play. Shorter grass will allow ground balls to travel farther than longer grass will. For the main playing areas, anywhere from 2 to 3 inches seems to work best for most people. (Personally, I like 2½ inches.) The infield and batter's "dirt" areas should be mown as low as possible[94] to cause the field to look like a "baseball" diamond. Whether you actually have grass in those areas is up to you. However, to keep the balls from rolling too fast through the white area to the yellow area,[95] and to cut down

---

92   An upside down Frisbee works well to hold and define the pitcher's stash of balls.
93   The scorekeeper decides. Only score a ball stuck in grass above the fence as being passed the fence if the ball is straddling the back edge of the fence.
94   Run the mowing deck flat on its own wheels if you can do that.
95   Stopping the dirt area three inches in front of the yellow line can mitigate the rolling issue somewhat if you really want to have infield dirt.

on the mud during wet days, I like to keep a little grass there. For the batter's boxes and the pitcher's mound, placing gravel in these areas will cut down on the mud, also. Or, in an emergency, placing old carpets in these smaller areas during the game (if there is too much mud) makes playing on wet days possible. If you use your field regularly, it should be mowed at least twice a week, otherwise, just before, or no more than one day before, you play, if possible.

- **Sticks, Stones, and Leaves** – Play as the ball lies. However, you should consider keeping the playing field free of sticks, stones, and leaves.

- Trees (and Bushes)

  o The scorekeeper makes the decisions regarding play affected by trees and bushes. To eliminate confusion, try to remove all trees and bushes that may affect play.

  o If the trunk of the tree is completely in foul territory closer than, or on, the extended yellow line (see the Field Plan), do the following:

    - If the batted ball contacts the trunk of the tree (below the first limb), it is a normal foul ball.

    - If the forward and/or upward motion of the ball stops within the limbs of the tree without passing through and the ball either stays in the tree or falls to the ground under the tree in fair territory, score a strike, but not a strikeout or a foul out.

    - If the forward and/or upward motion of the ball stops within the limbs of the tree without passing through and the ball falls to the ground in foul territory, score a foul ball and out(s) as the rules indicate.

    - If the forward and/or upward motion of the ball passes through the limbs of the tree and continues its forward and/or upward motion, play as normal (as if there were no tree).

  o If the trunk of the tree is in fair territory, straddling the foul line, or completely passed the yellow line in foul territory, do the following:

    - If the batted ball falls to the ground:

- If the ball contacts the tree above the first branch and does not hit the trunk:
    - If the ball stops in fair territory, score a fair ball.
    - If the ball stops in foul territory and not otherwise a fair ball, score a foul ball and out(s) as the rules indicate.
- However, if the ball contacts the trunk of the tree (below the first branch), even after contacting the tree elsewhere first:
    - If the trunk is completely in fair territory, score a fair ball and apply all other rules, playing the ball as it lies.
    - If the trunk is completely in foul territory, score a foul ball and out(s) as other rules indicate, playing the ball from the base of the tree.
    - If the trunk is straddling the foul line, play the ball as it lies as if there was no tree, applying all other rules.
- If the batted ball stays in the tree:
    - If it is obviously fair, score a homerun.
    - If it is obviously foul, score a strike, but no strikeout or foul out.
    - Otherwise,
        - If any part of the trunk of the tree is in fair territory, score a homerun.
        - If the trunk of the tree is completely in foul territory, score as a foul ball out of play (no strikeout or foul out).
        - If the location of the ball is uncertain or it is uncertain regarding which tree is holding the ball, the options being either fair or foul, the batter can use the options outlined in Appendix E.

Chapter 3 "Fundamentals"—Technical Issues 53

- **Clothing, Players**[96] (other than the pitcher), and **Other Obstructions** that are not part of the real estate and are owned by players
  - Keep clothing, extra people, etc. off the field to simplify things.[97]
  - If the personal property owned by a player of the batting team is the obstruction, play as the ball lies.
  - If a member of the batting team is the obstruction, including stand-in base runners, play from that part of the player closest to home plate, or the point of contact, whichever is closer. Or, if the obstruction does not take control of or throw the ball,[98] the batter may accept the lie of the ball.
  - If a member of, or personal property owned by a player of, the pitching team, or anyone else, including stand-in base runners,[99] treat as interference; the batter can use the options outlined in Appendix E.
  - Players who are out of bounds or in the dugout are treated as spectators (below).
  - The ball is dead when it contacts the catcher, regardless of which team he represents, or whether he represents any team at all.
- Spectators[100] and Ground Animals
  - If the spectator or ground animal is on or touching the playing surface:[101]
    - If in a dugout, a bullpen area, or an area designated for players to sit, the ball is dead. Score a normal foul ball.
    - Mark the position of the ball at the location of the ball on the ground or location of the back foot of the spectator or the chair he might be sitting in, whichever is farther from home plate.
    - However, if a spectator or animal gains control of the ball and begins to move it around on the playing surface, mark the place where it was picked up.

---

96   Including stand-in base runners (chapter 2).
97   Excepting stand-in base runners (chapter 2).
98   See the spectator rules below.
99   Not the pitcher himself or clothing he is wearing; he is supposed to be fielding the ball. Any personal property on the playing field that is not owned by the batting team is assumed by these rules to be owned by the pitching team.
100 If spectators are causing problems, they should be warned or asked to leave.
101 In fair or foul territory

- With either method, it is interference, and the batter has several options. See Appendix E.

- If the spectator (or ground animal) is completely out of play (or leaning across the barrier), not touching the playing surface:
    - If the spectator is in fair territory and the batted ball is a fair ball:
        - If the batted ball is touched or caught by the spectator without ever contacting the playing surface (a fly ball) and is taken out of play, score a homerun.
        - If the batted ball is touched or caught by the spectator and taken out of play after the ball bounces on the playing surface in play, score a triple.
        - If the batted ball is touched (or batted) by a forward-leaning spectator and remains on the playing surface, play as if the spectator did not touch it. Play as it lies. (If the spectator throws the ball, score as a catch taken out of play above).
    - If the spectator is in foul territory:
        - If the batted ball is touched or caught by the spectator without ever contacting the playing surface (a fly ball) and is taken out of play, record a strike, no strikeout or foul out.
        - If the batted ball is touched or caught by the spectator and taken out of play after the ball bounces on the playing surface in play:
            - If a foul ball, record a strike, no strikeout or foul out.
            - If otherwise a fair ball, score a double, three base advance (2B–3).
        - If the batted ball is touched (or batted) by a forward-leaning spectator and remains on the playing surface, play as if the spectator did not touch it. Play as it lies. (If the spectator throws the ball, score as a catch taken out of play above).
        - Quadruple play situations adjust these rules for foul balls.

- **Flying Animals** – Play the ball as it lies as if it were not touched. However, if a flying animal gains control of the ball and begins to move it around, it is interference, and the batter has several options. See Appendix E.

- Wires
    - If the wire is completely passed the yellow line:
        - If the ball comes down to the ground, play the lie of the ball as if the obstruction was not there.
        - If the ball is dead above the ground ("never" comes down):
            - If it is obviously fair, score a homerun.
            - If it is obviously foul, score a strike, but no strikeout or foul out.
            - If the location of the ball is uncertain, the options being either fair or foul, the batter can use the options outlined in Appendix E.
    - If any part of the wire is inside the yellow line in fair territory:
        - If either the forward or upward motion of the ball is stopped by the wire without passing through and the ball either stays on the wire, or falls to the ground inside the yellow line in fair territory, score a strike, but not a strikeout or a foul out.
        - If either the forward or upward motion of the ball is stopped by the wire without passing through and the ball falls to the ground in foul territory, score a foul ball and out(s) as the rules indicate.
        - If the forward and/or upward motion of the ball contacts the wire, passes through, and continues both its forward and upward motion passed the yellow line inclusive, play as normal (as if there was no wire).

- **Homerun Barrier** – See the "Black Line" rules in the "Base-Hit" section above.

Chapter 4

A "Level" Playing Field

This game can be played "straight up"[102]; that is, without any handicaps whatsoever. However, to provide the most fun for the most people, the players should be handicapped to allow the less experienced players a chance to participate on a more equal level with the advanced players.

When older players play with younger players, the younger ones learn how the game works, and spiritual and mental growth occurs. Yes, it is possible to become serious in this game, and that can be all right within its sphere and with proper sportsmanship, but the real joy comes through mentoring. These handicaps facilitate growth because they have the inherent ability to seamlessly challenge players to improve their skills. It is the recommendation of this author that these handicaps will enhance the experience of all.

These handicaps work best through the Random Roster Program because this individualizes the players. If you have set teams, the handicaps will be effective primarily team-by-team only as all the players will tend to share their team's win/loss record so that they basically will carry a team handicap. This is because they would be mostly all the same for all players on the same team.[103] I prefer the Random Teams/Random Rosters Program for handicaps. (See chapter 5).

102 See chapter 6 regarding other versions.
103 To get around this, there is a handicap system based on individual performance statistics, but this system is beyond the scope of this book.

All handicaps are dynamic. They change as the game progresses. Each player starts the game with his basic handicap (phase 1), which is then adjusted accordingly for hitting and for pitching. Adjust the pitcher's handicap up or down for each inning as indicated on the scoresheet in the "Runs Scored Per Inning" box for each inning (phase 2). Adjust the batter's handicap up or down for each time up, as indicated in the "Runs Scored Per Inning" box on the scoresheet (again, phase 2) and also as indicated in the slot box for each batter in each inning (phase 3).

When batters and pitchers change, the newly entered players enter the game with their pre-game handicap; the remaining players for both teams keep adjusting their handicaps as the game progresses without respect for the new player.

As stated above, the dynamics of the players' handicaps are divided into three different phases:

- **Phase 1 / The "Player Handicap"** – Each individual player carries his own handicap number into the beginning of the game. This handicap is based on each person's individual win/loss record.

    o If either the pitchers or the batters are dominating the league, the handicap levels may be adjusted and/or relaxed. Any such modifications will be indicated on, or through, the "Lineup Selection Worksheet" or through the scorekeeper's records.

    o Rookies – Until a player has played a few games, we don't know what his handicap should be and, therefore, a basic starting handicap of 35 for a rookie is assumed.

    - As a pitcher, start him at 35 and adjust as normal.

    - For batting, in his first time up and until he gets his first base hit (walks and HBP don't count) his starting handicap is 15. Do not make any adjustments to his 15 handicap until he gets his first base hit.

        o After his first base hit, his handicap rises to 35. Set it at 35 and adjust as normal.

        o After his second base hit, his handicap rises to 50. Set it at 50 and adjust as normal.

        o If he hits a homerun, set his handicap at 50 (regardless of any other hits) and adjust as normal.

        o If he hits a second homerun, set his handicap at 65 (regardless of any other hits) and adjust as normal.

    o If a player is on the winning team often, his handicap gets more challenging. If he is frequently on the losing team, his handicap gets easier.

The handicaps will seek equilibrium and settle at or near the players' true handicap based on age and ability. At equilibrium each player will be playing approximately 50–50 on winning and losing teams, so no one should feel left out.

- ○ Write this handicap on the scoresheet in the "Dynamic HCP" box at the top of innings 1 and 2.

- **Phase 2 / The "Inning Handicap"** – This handicap number is adjusted cumulatively for each team after each inning based on the number of runs scored by that team in its previous inning batted.

  - ○ This adjustment has the effect of keeping the games close. Not only does this enhance the excitement of the game, but it increases and improves opportunities to teach unselfishness, where the hit and run play, the stolen base, and advancing the runner can be taught in critical game situations.
  - ○ Write this adjusted handicap on the scoresheet in the "Dynamic HCP" box at the top innings 3 through 10.

- **Phase 3 / The "Random Handicap"** – This number is also adjusted randomly each inning to prevent players from falling into a rut. This number is not cumulative and is built into the scoresheet. It is the same for both teams.

  - ○ Depending on the player's skill level and specific idiosyncrasies, some players will get a base hit every time at one handicap level, and make an out every time at the next higher handicap level. Making the handicaps dynamic and random during the game helps reduce a situation in which the player is alternating between 0 for 5 and 5 for 5 games.
  - ○ Make the adjustment mentally and apply to the large "Dynamic Handicaps" box to the right on the scoresheet as the players bat.

The handicaps may sound artificial in some respects. However, no matter how easy any given player's handicap may appear at the beginning of an at bat, the players still have to do it, and they still receive affirmation upon success. Even failures can be affirmed, if done correctly. This is important in baseball, and for life in general.

These handicaps will never reach perfection. Besides, no matter how difficult a player's handicap might become, the experienced player will adjust to circumstances and will still figure out ways to win more often than not. However, these handicaps will encourage such intelligent play (which is the goal) and, in spite of all this, will indeed have a tendency to "level the playing field" for the whole group of players.

With all this in mind, let's take a look at how this works.

Handicap Calculations, the Field Plan, and the Scoresheet

Use the "Scoresheet" and the "Field Plan" to control the flow of the game. All the handicap calculations and results, as well as the lineups and pitchers, are indicated there. Use the "Field Plan" to determine singles, doubles, triples, and homeruns based on the player's handicaps. There are colored lines that correspond to the color of the batters' handicaps.

If the ball is touching any line (except the foul line, which is always fair), unless an applicable rule states otherwise, the batter decides which side of the line will apply.[104]

The color of the letter on the "letter board" determines whether a hit or an out is recorded. If the batted ball is passed the line corresponding to his letter's color, score a base hit. (Remember, if it is touching the line, the batter decides which side of the line to use.)

The main (solid) color on the "letter board" determines what kind of base hit is scored, check the color of the indicators (such as "1B-2," see below). These colored indicators correspond to the color of the batter's power handicap based on the location of the ball.

Some scoresheet considerations are as follows:

- **Black and White** – The "white line" represents the line next to the bases and the base paths, and the "black line" represents the outfield "fence." The lines themselves are both colored black, both on the field[105] and on the scoresheet, but are easily distinguished from each other, the white line being much closer to home plate than the black line and right next to the white bases. The white line is called "white" in order to easily indicate the difference between the two lines in conversation. Please note that the white line skirts in front of the bases and does not quite reach the bases. The "white" line is actually indicated on the ball field with black markers. (The bases themselves are actually white.) Such is the situation regarding the black and the white.

    o It is necessary to note the difference between the indicators on the field plan for the black power handicap and the white power handicap, as the white color, if used on the field plan, would fade into the background and would appear invisible. The black power handicap indicators are written in black with a box around them. The white power handicap indicators are also written in black, but are underlined instead of boxed.

- **Orange and Turquoise** – These indicators are displayed on the field plan using both colors and have a box around them. The same indicators apply for both colors.

---

104   Stretch a tape measure between the field markers to determine the lay of the ball with respect to any important line on the field. Use both edges of the markers, if necessary.
105   Unless, of course, you paint your fence a different color, such as green.

- When the batter hits a fair ball:

    o If the ball is passed the line required for a base hit (using the batter's[106] letter color handicap), note the closest line that the ball has passed. In the area between that line and the next line not passed, you will find on the field plan colored indicators, such as 1B–2 = single, the batter stops at first base, base runners advance 2 bases; 1B–0 = single, the batter stops at first base, any runner on third base scores, other runners are forced; 2B–2 = double, the batter stops at second base, base runners advance 2 bases; 2B–3 = double, the batter stops at second base, all base runners score; 3B = triple, the batter stops at third base, all base runners score; HR = homerun, everyone scores. Read from the indicator that matches the batter's solid color handicap and score the play accordingly.

    o If the ball is passed the line required for the batter to record a base hit and there is no indicator matching his solid color, score a 1B–1 = single (the default), the batter stops at first base, base runners advance 1 base.

    o "2B–2•," "1B–2•," or "1B–1•" – If a dot is indicated, the following applies: if this is the fourth batter of the inning and, at the start of the play, there is a runner on first or second base, he can try to score (by advancing one extra base only) on a base running conversion (above). For "2B–2•," pitch from the back mound. For "1B–2•" and "1B–1•," pitch from the close mound. Refer to the base running conversion rules above for more details.

Handicaps for Batters

The batter's handicap is divided into three aspects: Hitting, Power, and Strike Zone:

- The **hitting handicap** is indicated by the letters with their various colors. The letters indicate how far the batter needs to hit the ball to score a base hit, the color of the letter corresponding with the color of the goal line. It also affects whether the pitcher can record a strike on balls swung at that are out of the strike zone.[107] These letters' colors are indicated on the Field Plan, and the specifics are outlined above. The batter's hitting handicap is indicated on the scoresheet in the hitter's "Dynamic Handicap" section. See below for details of the various hitting handicaps. (If desired, the batter can substitute the pitcher's letter/color board. Some exceptions apply. See pitcher's handicaps below.)

---

106 Or the pitcher's, if the batter chooses to use pitcher's letter (color) board.
107 As an example, for some players, the batter's abilities do not yet include the ability to be pitch selective. Therefore, some handicap levels will not allow a strike unless the pitch is in the strike zone, even if the batter swings at the pitch. (See below for details.)

- The **power handicap** is indicated by the solid color. These colors indicate how far the batter needs to hit the ball to hit a homerun or to score other types of base hits. These are indicated on the Field Plan. The power colors also indicate what type of ball the pitcher may pitch to the batter (see below, and also the section on "Equipment"). The batter's power handicap is indicated on the scoresheet in the hitter's "Dynamic Handicap" section. (If desired, the batter can substitute the pitcher's letter/color board. Some exceptions apply. See pitcher's handicaps below.)

    - For power handicap colors of purple, white, yellow, grey, red, or blue use the regular white game balls. The homerun line corresponds to the line with the same color and the batted ball can roll or bounce across the homerun line to score a homerun. Extra base hits are scored according to the field plan. Score the play from the batted ball's farthest advance.[108] If it contacts the homerun barrier, score a homerun.

    - For power handicap colors of black, orange, and turquoise (see below), the homerun line is the fence ("black") and the type of ball used corresponds to color of the handicap marker, except that the black handicap uses the regular white balls.[109] Extra base hits are scored according to the field plan. Play the ball as it lies, even if it bounces back toward the infield.[110] The batted ball must clear the fence on the fly (without touching any ground beforehand) in order to score a homerun. (See the "Black Line" rules in the "Base-Hit" section above for more details.)

    - Orange and turquoise balls vary from the regular white game balls in texture (having holes in the plastic) and in firmness. They don't travel as far as the regular white game balls. The color of the ball can be indicated by the color of the plastic, the color of the stuffing if the plastic is a different color, or both.[111]

        - If the pitcher throws the wrong ball,[112] the batter has several options. See Appendix E.

---

108   Certain exceptions apply, particularly relating to obstructions.
109   Who wants to try to hit black balls?
110   Certain exceptions apply, particularly relating to obstructions.
111   Our turquoise balls have yellow plastic and turquoise stuffing that can be seen through the holes in the plastic. Our orange balls have orange plastic and orange stuffing. White balls with holes are easy to find in the stores and can be used with colored stuffing; just pay attention to the firmness. The turquoise balls have to be squeezable with the bare hand.
112   White or orange balls can be thrown to an orange handicap batter and any ball can be thrown to a turquoise handicap batter. Only white balls can be thrown in all the other types of handicaps.

- The **strike zone** handicap affects the strike zone boards. This line of handicaps will range anywhere from hitting off the tee to the big board straight up. They determine the size of the batter's strike zone and whether the pitcher can pitch freestyle or underhand only. They also govern the "Automatic Called Strike Three" as detailed below. The batter's strike zone handicap is indicated on the scoresheet under the hitter's "Dynamic Handicap" section.

Hitting Handicaps

- A – Batted balls that pass the red line on a fly or bounce are base hits. All other (fair) batted balls are outs to the fielder (default).

- B – In addition to above, batted balls that pass the grey line on a fly or bounce are base hits.

- C – In addition to above, batted balls that pass the yellow line on a fly or bounce are base hits.

- X – In addition to above, batted balls that pass the white line on a fly or bounce are base hits.

- D – In addition to above, batted balls that pass the purple line on a fly or bounce are base hits.

- E – In addition to above, batted balls that pass the pink line on a fly or bounce are base hits. Also, passed balls[113] are strikes, except you cannot strike out on a passed ball. The first 2 strikes can be a passed ball. Score passed balls after strike two as balls.

- F – In addition to above, all fair balls are base hits. The first strike can be a passed ball. After that, passed balls are balls.

- G – In addition to above, the batter may use either the thin (yellow) bat or the fat (orange) bat. All passed balls are balls. Check the scoresheet for a possible exemption from fouling out when using the can for a strike zone.

Handicaps for Pitchers

The pitcher's handicap is divided into two aspects: Hitting/Power and Strike Count.

---

[113] See the definition of "Passed Ball" above.

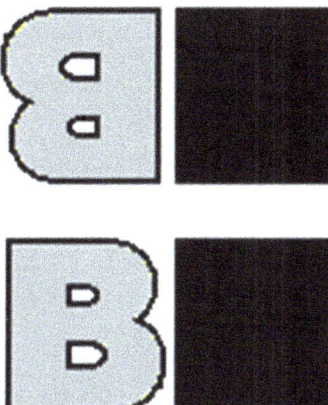

- The **hitting/power handicap** affects the letters and colors. The pitchers each have their own letter/color boards, similar to the batters. They work the same as the batter's letter/color board, except the batter can choose between using his own letter/color board and using the pitcher's letter/color board.

- The **strike count handicap** affects the number of strikes the batter has at the start of his plate appearance. These will range anywhere from plus 2 strikes to negative 2 strikes. It also affects quadruple plays on foul outs, and whether the ball count reverts to zero when a strike is recorded. The pitcher's strike count handicap and the batter's initial strike count are indicated on the scoresheet under the pitcher's dynamic handicap.

    o Look on the scoresheet under the column "Count." The abbreviations listed have the following meanings:

    - S +1 = The batter comes to bat with a strike count of positive 1.

    - S -2 = The batter comes to bat with a strike count of negative 2.

    - W = If the at bat results in a walk, use the Wildcard tee.

    - GGii = To record a strike, the pitcher must throw a strike regardless of whether the batter swings ("Gotta Get it in").

    - Hold = regular baseball count rules apply. The count starts with no balls and no strikes. The ball count holds (does not change) after recording a strike, which also always applies to any strike count that starts with -1 or lower.

    - None = The count starts with no balls and no strikes. The ball count reverts to zero after recording a strike, which also always applies to any count that starts with one strike or higher.

- 4xF = Quadruple Foul out. The batter and all runners are out. (See the section titled "The 'Double Play' and More," above).

Strike Zone Boards

- For boards that are straight up in the second basket, a called strike (batter does not swing) is an automatic strikeout ("Automatic Called Strike Three").

- Some handicaps require the pitcher to pitch underhand. See the "Dynamic Handicaps" chart on the scoresheet for an indication of which batter's handicaps require pitching underhand.

- For other handicaps the pitcher can choose either underhand or overhand, called "freestyle."

Chapter 5

The Commissioner's "Antics"— Administrative Considerations

Sometimes it becomes necessary for a player to leave the game early. Other times there are players who arrive after the game has started, and you don't really want to leave anyone out. This generally leaves the scorekeeper in a quandary about what to do while trying to keep the game both interesting and fair. You could simply cut off additions after the first pitch and allow new arrivals to wait to see if there will be any departures, thus resulting in the need for substitutions, but if you want to try to get people into the game, here are some suggestions that might help maintain an orderly way of accomplishing your goal. Everyone's situation is different, so please apply these suggestions as they work for you.

"Dead Ringer"/"Absent Player"

- If there are an odd number of players in the game, play an invisible player named "Dead Ringer" to even the number of players on each team. Dead Ringer plays as any regular player, except that he otherwise follows the "Absent Player" rules. Dead Ringer's pitching role is "none." Follow the rules for setting up the lineups on the "Lineup Selection Worksheet." Any live player can substitute for Dead Ringer. Follow the substitution and absent player rules in the "Absent Player-Withdrawals" (below). For more information on how to use Dead Ringer in a lineup see the "'Person' vs. 'Player' – the ambidextrous 'Two-player Person'" rules above and also refer to Appendix C regarding the lineup selection process.

- If, during the pitch, the batter takes his batting position (or strides, sits, or stands) with all of both feet outside of the batter's box inclusive, he is an "absent player." Treat the batter as "trying for a tee shot" (see above).[114]

- When pitching to Dead Ringer or any "absent batter":
  - The absent batter uses his own letter board. Do not use the pitcher's letter board.
  - Suspend the automatic called strike three rule, but use the strike zone boards that his handicap specifies.
  - Use the "absent batter" line on the walk chart unless the batter is present and places the tee, in which case use the regular walk rules. (See the walk, tee, and "Try for a Tee Shot" rules above).

- When batting against Dead Ringer or any "absent pitcher":
  - The batter chooses between his letter board and the pitcher's.
  - Accept a walk from the walk chart for a "4xF Pitcher." This would be a 1-base walk runner's forced (1W–0) and represents the batter's first plate appearance of his time up.
  - Then bat from the tee using the rules for hitting off the tee (above) using the count indicated by the pitcher's strike count handicap. This is the batter's second plate appearance of his time up. (Under certain circumstances, he might use the wildcard tee.)

- If Dead Ringer pitches to himself (or an absent pitcher pitches to an absent batter), score a walk from the walk chart, drawing the strike count from the pitcher's handicap and the number of baskets from the batter's handicap.

---

114   Note: Every player in the game fills a batting slot, but no one ever has to bat. This is to satisfy the needs of people with certain disabilities, or those who just prefer to pitch only. For these players, you should consider giving them the "long relief" pitching role to increase their opportunity to actually participate. When their turn comes to bat, they bat as an absent batter. If, when batting, they only want to hit off the tee, they can use the "Try For a Tee Shot" procedures. If you have two people, one who wants to bat and another who wants to pitch, let them substitute for each other. Then for the record, use the one whose performance during the game most closely represents their team's performance. See "Win/Loss Times Up" rules below.

Chapter 5   The Commissioner's "Antics"—Administrative Considerations

Ignore any Wildcard indicators. Do not bat the second time that normally follows a walk.

Substitution

- Remember, the maximum number of players for both teams together is 12 batters and 12 pitchers. Unfortunately, someone might have to wait until the next game.[115] See "'All-Star' Game Format" (below) for additional ideas. If using more players becomes a normal activity, modifying the standard scoresheet to add slots is a possible solution, if you are so inclined.

- Do not list any substitute in more than one slot and on more than one team at the same time unless he is replacing someone who is in more than one slot or he qualifies as an ambidextrous "Two-player Person" (above), and don't push that if Dead Ringer is playing, for he can simply play for Dead Ringer.

- If a player arrives after the game has started,[116]

  o First, fill in for any vacated players (including Dead Ringer) or for players (including doubled ambidextrous players) who are filling up more than one slot (more than one time up to bat in each inning), filling in as the need arises (as they come to bat).

  o Second, if all your vacated players (including Dead Ringer, doubled ambidextrous players, and players batting in more than one slot) are replaced or accounted for:

    - What follows can complicate your scoresheet, so I don't recommend it. But if you are so inclined, you may add slots to each team to accommodate your extra players up to 6 total both sides (using batting slots 5 and/or 6 on the scoresheet, if available and applicable). Use discretion.[117]

    - If you do add slots, fill those in as the need arises, live players first and then with Dead Ringer, as necessary. (Dead Ringer may end up jumping teams and playing a partial game for each team, which is OK.)

---

115   You might need to set up a system to determine a priority for whose turn it might be to wait, maybe giving playing priority to the person with the most games sat out per games showed up (GSO/GSU).
116   If more than one person arrives at the same time, place each person one at a time in random order. The scorekeeper may override the randomness of this order in his better judgment, maybe giving playing priority to the person with the most games sat out per games showed up (GSO/GSU) or giving priority to the youngest first (or whatever).
117   My personal inclination is to use slots 5 and/or 6 only when I have more than 8 players at the start of the game and not change the number of slots during the game.

- I suggest that you not adjust the pitching arrangements except to replace or substitute for pitchers as the need arises, as adding pitching slots can become complicated to administer.
  - "Win/Loss Times Up" – For keeping track of players' win/loss records, count players officially in the game as those who batted the most ("times up"). For example, if there are 8 players in the game (4 on each side), and someone substituted for one time up, the 4 players for each team who had the most times up are those of record. If there is a tie, then evaluate in the following way. If his team won, use the player that contributed most to his team's win. If his team lost, record the player who did the least to contribute to a conceivable win. If Dead Ringer plays on both teams, he could end up with a record for each team, for neither team, or for either one or the other. In the end, there should be the same number of players with a record as there were batting slots for each team at the start of the game. This decision can be subjective, in that both pitching and hitting need to be evaluated.[118]

Absent Player/Withdrawals[119]

- Do not use Dead Ringer as a substitute or as a pinch hitter. It is much easier to let the absent batter bat absentee. However, if you have players sitting on the bench hoping to play, do not hesitate to allow such players to bat for the absent player.

- If the batter misses his turn at bat or otherwise withdraws from the game for any reason:
  - Assuming a qualifying substitute is available (someone not playing for either team and who desires to play), he can substitute for the departed batter. If the absent player does not return, the slot belongs to the substitute; otherwise, the slated batter can have his slot back when he returns. If the absent player returns while his substitute is batting, the substitute is allowed to finish his time up, the now-returned player can bat in his next turn, and the substitute is available for reassignment. If the substitute does

---

118   A situation can develop, particularly in a 5-person game, where some players (including ambidextrous players) bat twice as much as some others. Special record keeping is recommended in such a situation. Count such player(s) as playing two games instead of one in their win/loss records.

119   Note: You will probably only have a substitute available when you have more than 12 people who want to play or you have had a late player arrive but have not been able to reset the lineups yet or you choose not to increase the number of slots. See "player arrives after the game has started" below.

not have a player handicap of his own, his default handicap is 15+. (See "Rookies" in chapter 3.)

- o If that doesn't result in a new batter, pitch to him as an "absent batter" (above).

- If the pitcher misses his turn to pitch, becomes weak,[120] or otherwise withdraws from the game for any reason:

- o Assuming a qualifying substitute is available (someone not playing for either team and who desires to play), he can finish the departed pitcher's inning. If the absent pitcher does not return, the slot belongs to the substitute; otherwise, the slated pitcher gets his slot back when he returns. If the absent player returns while his substitute is pitching, the substitute is allowed to finish the inning, the now-returned player can pitch in his next turn, and the substitute is available for reassignment. If the substitute does not have a player handicap of his own, his default handicap is 35.

- o If that doesn't result in a new pitcher, bat as facing an "absent pitcher" (above).

- Note: A situation can develop when more than one player may be absent at the same time. If that happens, just keep playing through it. However, if each team has a player absent who is not returning,[121] and only if you have more than 4 slots in use (each side), it may be expedient to reduce the teams by one player each, starting with the player(s) who have been out the longest (skipping them in the lineups). If anyone does come back, put them back in the game and add one player to the other team also. It is not recommended, and you can only do this when playing random rosters, but if you want, having player(s) cross over to the other team can overcome a lopsided situation. When you do this, tallying the totals at the end of the game will be affected. Pay attention to which team, if any, will be affected by the player's win/loss record. For more information, see "Win/Loss Times Up" and "Substitution" rules (above).[122]

"All-Star" Game Format

If you have 10 or 12 players and everybody wants to have a chance to pitch,[123] you can use an "All-Star" format in which each player pitches one inning. The scoresheet has slots for up to 6 pitchers per side to handle so many pitchers. (Don't break up innings by

---

120   See the "Weak Pitcher" rules.
121   You can count Dead Ringer as one of these.
122   If this situation develops, don't be concerned with trying to keep the two sides even in ability. That will all play out in future games anyway. Right now, your main concern is for everyone to have a good time playing ball.
123   This can happen if you have a number of visitors.

having more than one pitcher pitch in the same inning, except when someone is unable to continue.) If you have even more players than that, you will have to scramble. If you really want to deal with all this, you can substitute batters during the game to give everyone a chance to bat. However, not everyone can pitch a full inning with so many players. You will need to decide who plays full time and who plays part time. Maybe some bat without pitching and some pitch without batting.[124]

"Season"

There are different formats for playing a season, should you so desire. If you are going to have a formal league with roster sizes in excess of four, I suggest using the standard eight-player game format for the best effects regarding the game itself. Your league can have its own rules for substitutions during the game. Different season formats can be as follows:

- Round Robin – Most professional baseball leagues play (or used to play[125]) a round robin. This requires scheduling and a set number of games, which in itself can be a source of stress to try to fill.

- Challenge Season

  o I like the challenge season in which teams schedule their own games on a challenge basis. This eliminates the stress of trying to meet a specific number of games or trying to make a schedule. Determine a division winner by games won less games lost ("games over 500") and break ties by dividing the games won by the total number of games played (win/loss percentage).[126] In this scenario the teams who play the most will have a slight advantage.

  o In the challenge season, when teams make their own arrangements regarding whom they play, teams may have a tendency to focus on certain opponents. In order to encourage teams to play a variety of opponents (thus widening the cross section and spreading the fun), limit the W/L record between any two opponents to plus or minus three games over 500. For example, a 4–0 record between the Red Fox and the Falcons will show as 3–0 in the standings and 5–1 will show 4–1 in the standings and vice

---

124   If you have more than 12 people, it is best to play two games if you have enough fields, or a double header (consecutively) if you have enough time. The doubleheader can be tricky if everyone wants to play in both games, so you might have to have a system regarding who has to sit out, whether you play two games or just one, maybe giving playing priority to the person with the most games sat out per games showed up (GSO/GSU). One such system could be to combine players such that some bat only and some pitch only, or, maybe, to change batters after the 4th inning, or whatever.
125   Before the inter-divisional and inter-league formats.
126   Break ties between "500" teams by games played, giving priority to the most games played.

versa.[127] (This rule is not needed if the teams are selected randomly or are playing a round robin.)

- Random Season – My favorite is the random season. This is similar to, and operates the same as, the challenge season except the teams play each other at random. This usually works best with the random rosters (below).

- Set Rosters – Obviously, if you have enough players in your league, you can set up specific teams with set rosters of players and play a season. The rosters can vary in size from 1 to as many as you want, depending on your league rules. This is the situation in which I suggest playing exactly 8 total players in a game, but you can set the number at any size you want.

- Random Rosters – I have discovered that the most fun with a league of up to a dozen or so people is to combine the Random Season with Random Rosters (which is the perspective from which I am writing this book). You have a "league" of fictitious teams, maybe, with a theme in which all the teams are named after animals, or something. Then you set a time and place, and it doesn't matter who or how many people come to play. The teams for each game are chosen at random and you use the "Lineup Selection Worksheet" to set your lineups.[128] This will randomize your league in such a way that everyone can claim to be a member of the league champion at the end of the season and fun is had by all.

"World Series"

Play a "world series" to add excitement to the year, especially in October after your season ends. To play a series of seven games between the same two teams at the end of the season places a cherry on the top of the summer and punctuates meaning into a long season. Everything done all season long distills down to this one focal point; this climax of wit, skill, and effort. Carry the league scenario (such as random rosters, or whatever you have been using) into the postseason. As a suggestion, use the top two teams, the league champion against one wildcard, with the league champion taking home field advantage, or, if you want more teams in the postseason, use your own wildcard selection process.

---

127   Do not remove any losses from the dominant team. Instead, only take wins away from them, and only take losses away from the recessive team. If you make a 6–2 record into a 3–0 record, you have cut off any progress made by the recessive team. Instead, make a 6–2 record 5–2; and make a 5–15 record 5–8, etc.
128   You don't have to be tied to 8 players per game.

Sample Standings for a Typical Random Team/Random Roster Season

11/4/2013

2013 Miniature Baseball	W	L	Pct.	GB	W.Card
1 Falcons	6	2	0.750	--	☺
2 White Fox	5	3	0.625	1	--
3 Flamingos	4	3	0.571	1½	½
4 ~~Dragonflies~~	~~3~~	~~3~~	~~0.500~~	~~2~~	~~1~~
5 ~~Cardinals~~	~~2~~	~~2~~	~~0.500~~	~~2~~	~~1~~
6 ~~Scorpions~~	~~1~~	~~1~~	~~0.500~~	~~2~~	~~1~~
~~Red Fox~~	~~1~~	~~1~~	~~0.500~~	~~2~~	~~1~~
8 ~~Orioles~~	~~2~~	~~4~~	~~0.333~~	~~3~~	~~2~~
~~Cottontails~~	~~2~~	~~4~~	~~0.333~~	~~3~~	~~2~~
10 ~~Blackhawks*~~	~~3~~	~~6~~	~~0.333~~	~~3½~~	~~2½~~

* Defending champions

Last 11:
- Nov 3: WS5: White Fox 7, Falcons 6, 11 inn. W.Fox WIN 4-1 !
- Oct 21: WS4: White Fox 5, Falcons 4, White Fox lead 3-1
- Oct 20: WS3: White Fox 3, Falcons 2, White Fox lead 2-1
- Oct 7: WS2: White Fox 6, Falcons 2, Series tied at 1
- Oct 3: WS1: Falcons 5, White Fox 4, Falcons lead 1-0
- Sep 23: Dragonflies 3, White Fox 2
- Sep 16: Flamingos 3, Blackhawks 1
- Sep 9: Cardinals 6, Flamingos 4
- Sep 5: Cardinals 7, Dragonflies 5
- Sep 2: Orioles 3, Dragonflies 2
- Aug 29: Dragonflies 3, Orioles 0

Falcons
1 White Fox
2 Flamingos
3 DragCardScorRed
4 OrioCott
5 Blackhawks*

Refer to the sample final standings above for the 2013 season. Some overall league statistics for this season are as follows: ERA = 4.25; Batting Average = .355; OBP = .424; Slugging % = .648; OPS = 1.072; Total HR per Game = 2.40; HR per 1000 PA = 60; and Total Runs per Game = 8.38.

Chapter 6

You Be the Boss—Other Versions

The rules listed above are not the only way this game can be played. I have shown you the way they have worked for me. They can be considered complicated by some standards, but the essence of the game is the bat and the ball. So feel free to improvise any way you would like. The possibilities are endless. I can only make a very limited number of suggestions in this context, but let me set forth some examples. To repeat what was said earlier in the book (chapter 4), the dynamics of the players' handicaps can be divided into three different adjustment phases or categories:

- **The Player Handicap** – Each individual player carries his own handicap number into the beginning of the game. This handicap is based on each person's individual win/loss record.

- **The Inning Handicap** – This handicap number is then adjusted for each team after each inning based on the number of runs scored by that team in its previous inning batted.

- **The Random Handicap** – This number is also adjusted randomly each inning to prevent players from falling into a rut.

Each of these can be adjusted and combined differently to provide different versions of the basic field game, for those who prefer something different. Some possibilities are listed below. You may be able to add some of your own.

The Bare Bones Static Version

There is the option to play without handicapping the individual players for their various abilities. In the static version, everyone has the same beginning handicap number that never changes during the game (adjustment category 1, above). These are not individualized, but everyone uses the same number.

There are several advantages to this in that you don't have to give each batter a letter board when he bats, you don't need to keep changing the strike zone boards during the game, and you don't have to keep win/loss records (or even any records at all) if you don't want to. However, some of your players will possibly become discouraged and feel left out if they are not able to participate in the game at a "normal" level, such as getting base hits, driving in runs, or getting batters out while pitching. In addition, your better players may become bored because it is too easy.

However, if you really want to play without using handicaps, I suggest several options (below). Analyze the general abilities of all your players and choose a single number that will fit as closely as possible all your players corporately. Feel free to make adjustments as you prefer.

- For advanced players (the default), all players use the handicap number 50.
    - This will place all batters as Black-C, big board down. The base hit line is the yellow line, the homerun line is the fence, and the pitcher can pitch freestyle. The automatic called strike three feature is not needed.
    - All pitchers are GLD (Gold), "balls hold" (the same as regular baseball count rules). The pitcher's alternate handicap is not needed.
- For intermediate players (ages 8 and older, or inexperienced players), all players use the handicap number 40.
    - This will place all batters as Black-X, no strike zone boards. The base hit line is the white line, the homerun line is the fence, and the pitcher can pitch freestyle. The automatic called strike three feature is not needed.
    - All pitchers are WHT (White), "no count" (the ball count restarts at zero when a strike is recorded). The pitcher's alternate handicap is not needed.
- For beginning players (ages 0–7), all players use the handicap number 25.
    - This will place all batters as Red-D, front board. The base hit line is the purple line, the homerun line is the red line, and the pitcher must pitch underhand. The automatic called strike three feature is not needed.

- All pitchers are BLU (Blue), "strike one" (the ball count restarts at zero when a strike is recorded and the strike count starts at one). The pitcher's alternate handicap is not needed.

- For super-advanced players:
  - All batters use the handicap number 60. This will place all batters as Black-B, medium board up. The base hit line is the grey line, the homerun line is the fence, and the pitcher can pitch freestyle. The automatic called strike three feature is invoked.
  - All pitchers use the handicap number 50. This will place all pitchers as GLD (Gold), "balls hold" (the same as regular baseball count rules). The pitcher's alternate handicap is not needed.

- For "professional" players:
  - All batters use the handicap number 70. This will place all batters as Orange-A (orange balls), big board up. The base hit line is the red line, the homerun line is the fence, and the pitcher can pitch freestyle. The automatic called strike three feature is invoked.
  - All pitchers use the handicap number 50. This will place all pitchers as GLD (Gold), "balls hold" (the same as regular baseball count rules). The pitcher's alternate handicap is not used.

Alternative Versions

- **The "Pick-up" version** – In the "Pickup" version, all the players start with the same player handicaps across the board as given in the Static version above (adjustment category 1), except the inning handicaps change after each inning (adjustment category 2).

- **The "Enhanced Pick-up" Version** – As an alternative to the regular "Pick-up" version, you can also do the random adjustments (adjustment category 3).

- **The "Random Pick-up" Version** – As an alternative to the regular "Pick-up" version, you can do the random adjustments only and not change the handicaps after each inning (adjustment category 3).

- **The "Minimal Handicap" Version** – Each player starts with a personalized player handicap, but don't adjust each inning and don't use the random adjustments.

- **The "Adjusted Minimal" Version** – Add the inning and/or random adjustments.

- **The Fielders Game** – I have never done this, and I am too old for this now, but if you want to experiment, you could try playing the basic field game with nine fielders and a designated hitter, running and everything without using handicaps.

Chapter 7
Play Ball!

All this book can do at this point is to introduce you to the concept of the game. There is nothing that can beat firsthand experience. If this is your initial exposure to miniature baseball, you may benefit from talking to someone who has played this game before, or even better, experiencing a game firsthand. If you would like assistance, please contact me at CraigBarnes@AspectBooks.com.

Not everyone can play 9" hardball or even 12" softball. There are millions of people who, for one reason or another, cannot play these games. I believe we now have an alternative that will allow millions of people who long to play baseball to be able to participate in the greatest game ever created, through the medium of 5" small balls.

78 Small Ball: The Blessings of Miniature Baseball

Appendix A

Know the Score (The Scoresheet)

This illustration is in the public domain. You may copy it, give it to your friends, and use it for playing games, etc. Available at: http://glorylight.org/MiBaseball_Scoresheet.pdf or http://1ref.us/scoresheet Have fun!

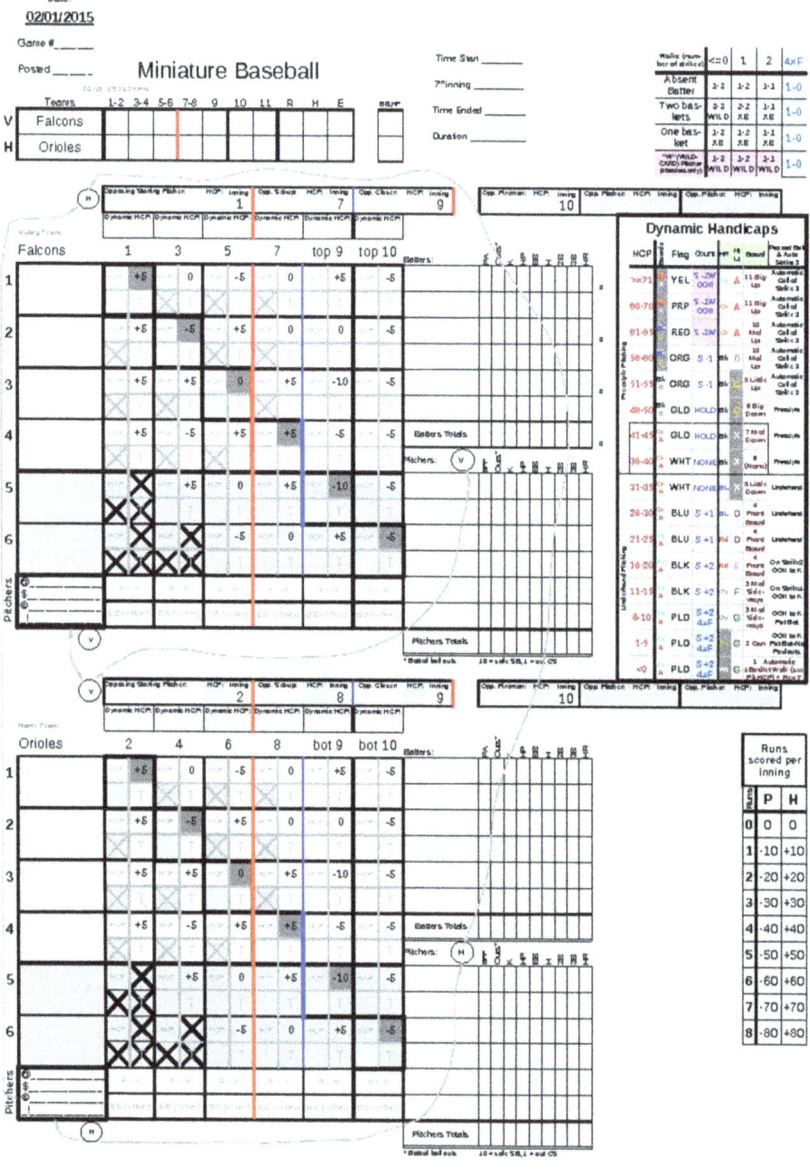

Appendix B

Dead Ringer and Ambidextrous Persons

(Especially With Less Than 8 People To Play)

If you have exactly 8 total persons to play a game, you are "good to go"—"play ball." However, most of the time you will not be that fortunate, so here are some ideas that should help.

In situations when you have 9 or more persons, if you don't have an ambidextrous person available to even up an odd number of players, play one Dead Ringer. (See also the "Dead Ringer" and "Absent Player" rules in chapter 5.)

If you have less than 8 persons, following is a plan whereby you can set up your teams using Dead Ringer and ambidextrous players.

- Ambidextrous Players – If you have any ambidextrous people not being used to full potential, include both ambidextrous players for as many ambidextrous people as you need to get to 8 players.[129] However, if applying all of your

---

[129] If you have more than enough ambidextrous persons, everything else being equal, playing priority should go to the player(s) with the highest combined games sat out per games showed up GSO/GSU. For the "extra" ambidextrous persons who will only be represented as one player, if they don't have a preference, use the highest GSO/GSU or flip a coin to choose which player will represent that person. You need to make this determination before you can make the lineups. (Yes, you should keep GSO information for each ambidextrous player, if not everybody.)

ambidextrous players gives you exactly 5 total players, do not use all of your ambidextrous players; let one sit out so you can play with 4 players. If more than 8, let some sit out so you can play with 8 players. If, after you have applied all of your ambidextrous players you are going to use, you are still short 8 players, go to the next step.

- Dead Ringer (after applying your ambidextrous players)

    o For 7 players, play one Dead Ringer to even up an odd number of players.

    o For 6 players, play one Dead Ringer on each team. Consulting your list of players present (incremented with your better players toward the bottom),[130] if Dead Ringer is in the middle, or inside of, the list of the six numbered players (not outside at the top or the bottom), move Dead Ringer to the top of the list and renumber from there, giving him both numbers 1 and 2 (effectively 2 Dead Ringers). (This will give you an even number of 8 players total.) Use the 1,2,2,1,1,2,2,1 (or the 2,1,1,2,2,1,1,2) label format. Do not use the 1,1,2,2,2,2,1,1 or 2,2,1,1,1,1,2,2 formats.

    o The 5-player scenario is the most difficult to administer, so don't use any ambidextrous players to get your fifth player; play with 4 players instead. If you have 5 persons exactly and no ambidextrous players to get above 5 players, you will use Dead Ringer. Go to the next step:

      - Label your 5 players 1,2,2,2,1 (or alternatively, 2,1,1,1,2). Do not label Dead Ringer, yet. See "Batters' Lineup" In Appendix C for more information:

      - Now apply Dead Ringer:

        o Consulting your list of players present, if Dead Ringer is in the middle, or inside of, the list of the five numbered players (not outside at the top or the bottom), add Dead Ringer to whichever team has three players, giving them four players. The other team will have two players.

        o If Dead Ringer is outside of the list, at either the top or the bottom, place 2 more Dead Ringers at the opposite end of the list. This will yield 3 Dead Ringers temporarily, which means there will be two on one team for the time being. Renumber for 8 players using the 1,2,2,1,1,2,2,1 (or the 2,1,1,2,2,1,1,2) label format.[131] Then eliminate the two Dead Ringers that are on the same team, leaving one team with two players.

---

130   See Appendix C for more information on how to list your players.
131   Not the 1,1,2,2,2,2,1,1 or the 2,2,1,1,1,1,2,2 formats.

- Then double-up the team with two players.
- Either scenario will give you an even number of 8 players total.

  o For 4 players, play with who you have. (This will give you an even number of 4 players, total. Each player will come to bat twice in each inning/half-inning.)

  o The 3-player scenario is the second most difficult to administer, so don't use any ambidextrous players to get your third player. Play with 2 players instead. If you have 3 persons exactly, play one Dead Ringer to even up the teams. (This will give you an even number of 4 players total. Each player will bat twice in each inning/half-inning.)

  o For 2 players, play with who you have. (This will give you an even number of 2 players, total. With two persons, this is a normal game. If you are an ambidextrous person playing against yourself, you will be alternating between hitting off the tee and pitching to the baskets, which is good practice. Each player will come to bat four times in each inning/half-inning.)

  o For 1 player, play one Dead Ringer to even up the teams. (This is basically a practice session, for all you will be doing is pitching to the baskets and hitting off the tee. But the question remains: Can you beat Dead Ringer? Or will Dead Ringer "walk all over you"?)

When you calculate your lineups, you need not be concerned at this point about ambidextrous players playing on the same team, except those on the same team should be pitching in the "backup" role.

Appendix C

The Lineup Selection Worksheet

In the random roster scenario especially, the selection of the lineups can be a critical aspect of the game, particularly with respect to the determination of who gets to pitch. Even in a standard four-player-per-team lineup, not all four players are likely to be able to pitch during the game, as there are generally only three pitchers who are scheduled to pitch, with one of those pitching only if the game is tied after regulation innings. I have some ideas that have worked in the past, so here are some of my recommendations.

One alternative is to pull the names out of a baseball cap or to use a random number generator application on your cell phone. These methods will save time, but you are likely to end up with more lopsided games if you do that, thus spoiling your attempts to teach the finer points of the game. The dice method recommended here actually skews the pitching a little toward your skilled players so as to keep things more on an "even keel." Your pitching is very important. One bad pitcher can spoil your game. There are opportunities to allow your novice players to learn to pitch, although somewhat less often than your advanced players. You may decide you are happy to take a little extra time to set up your lineups. (You might even choose to assign your novice pitchers to the "specialist" role to relieve some of the pressure on them.)

With that in mind, I recommend the following program.

Batters' Lineup

The objective of setting up the batters' lineup is to align the teams as evenly in ability as possible. We use the individual players' win/loss records to accomplish this. You will then use these lineups as a basis for selecting your pitchers.

Follow these procedures to determine your batting lineups:

- List all the players in your "league" or group in order, with the most games below 500 on the top to the most games above 500 on the bottom—i.e. your better players toward the bottom. (If you want, you really only need to list those who are actually present.[132]) Their pitching preference numbers (see below) should also be indicated next to their name.

- Cross off the list those who are not present, or circle those who are present. (Obviously, you can skip this step if you have listed only those who are present.)

- Place a "1" or a "2" next to the name of each of those present to indicate whether they are on the visiting team or the home team respectively. Do this in a "1,2,2,1,1,2,2,1..." format (alternating[133] from game to game with a 2,1,1,2,2,1,1,2,... format) as you go down the list of those present. This will effectively even out the abilities for the two teams.

  - Note: As the players accumulate win/loss records, they will shift around and you will eventually have a mixture of players on the different teams. However, to mix things up yourself, if you feel the need, you can substitute the format "1,1,2,2,2,2,1,1"[134] occasionally when the situation presents itself. One caveat with this format is it only works with 8 total players.[135]

- List in the lineups section on this worksheet, and also later on the "scoresheet," those players that apply to each team in the order you started with (by win/loss record, with your better players toward the bottom). This will establish your batting lineups and also the slot numbers you need for determining the pitchers.

Pitchers' Lineup

One could simply rotate the pitchers as they do in baseball, which is done because pitchers get tired and need to rest. Since, in miniature baseball, pitchers do not get tired, the rotation aspect can become rather superfluous. However, rotating pitchers also involves some additional record keeping over and above that which I have already recommended. You can try rotation if you like, but I prefer to do it randomly, because when using the ran-

---

132   If you computerize this, you will want to print out a list of all of them unless you know before printing who will be present.
133   The alternation can be effective if done randomly.
134   Alternating from game to game with a "2,2,1,1,1,1,2,2" format.
135   This will also most likely affect whether ambidextrous players play on the same team.

dom rosters, I don't always know who is going to show up for a game, thus complicating the record keeping for a pitching rotation.

The "menu" of pitching roles are as follows (with the identifying numbers shown for each role):

- Starter (1) – Starting pitchers pitch innings 1–6.

- Relief (2) – Relief pitchers pitch innings 7–9.

- Fireman (3) – Firemen pitch innings 10–11.

- Setup (4) – Setup pitchers pitch innings 7–8.

- Closer (5) – Closers pitch the 9th inning, save situations notwithstanding.

- Anything (6) – Most people fall into this role. They don't have a preference.

- Long relief (7) – Long relief pitchers also pitch innings 7–9, but with a higher priority. This role is generally reserved for visitors or other players you want to make sure they have a chance to pitch.

- Specialist (8) – Specialists also pitch the 9th inning, but with a lower priority. The specialist role is generally reserved for those who are learning how to pitch.

- Backup (9) – The backup role is for pitchers who want to pitch only if they are needed to fill a pitching slot. Ambidextrous players, when playing on opposite teams, also take the backup role.

- None (0) – These pitchers never actually pitch, unless they temporarily change their minds. Instead, if they are actually "called" on to pitch, they pitch absentee and follow the "Absent Player-Withdrawals" rules in chapter 5. This role is generally reserved for those who are physically incapable of pitching or for steadfast refusal. For example, Dead Ringer takes this role. However, this role is not available to ambidextrous players.

Setup, closer, and specialist pitchers work together. If you have a setup, closer, and/or a specialist pitcher activated in the game, the relief role is deleted and the counterpart setup/closer/specialist tandem is substituted. However, all pitchers can sometimes be called on to pitch in any of the roles other than what they have chosen as their priority.

After I have the batting order set up, I like to select the pitchers randomly based on the team's batting lineup and what the pitchers' individual preferred roles are. Therefore, I recommend the following procedures to determine your pitchers.

Start with the visiting team, and for each player, perform steps one and two first:

1. Roll two standard six-sided dice[136] and add them together. Consult the left side of the "slot chart" (below) and read the first result for the number rolled on your dice. This resulting number represents the slot in the batting lineup on the scoresheet for each team respectively, which in turn, represents a player you will be working with to determine his pitching activity during the game. If the first slot number drawn is already used, or is not available, then read the second number, etc., until you find an available slot number. Note the player's role number and go to the next step.

2. On the "pitching chart," note the role preference for each player/person and consult the "preference chart" (below). Start at the left of his role preference column and read the results until you encounter an available role for this player in this game. Write his name and role number in that role slot on the "pitching chart." If you encounter the words "wait1" or "wait2", etc. (or "W1", "W2", etc.), write both his name and his role number in the appropriate "wait" section ("W1", "W2", etc.) on the "pitching chart." Then do the next player.

3. When all the players for that team are finished with respect to steps 1 and 2, then look at the "wait" list. If there are any names listed in the "wait" list, start at the top of that list, beginning with "wait1" and consult the "preference chart" again from where you left off (to the right of the line). Keep going down the list through "wait1" and "wait2", etc., until you find an unfilled role in the "pitching chart." When all of the players in the "wait" list are assigned, you are ready to enter the pitchers on the "scoresheet." (If you have not already done so, you may enter the batters at this time also.)

4. Perform steps 1–3 for the home team as you did for the visiting team. Now you are ready to ... play ball!

---

136   By the way, there are cell phone applications that will simulate dice.

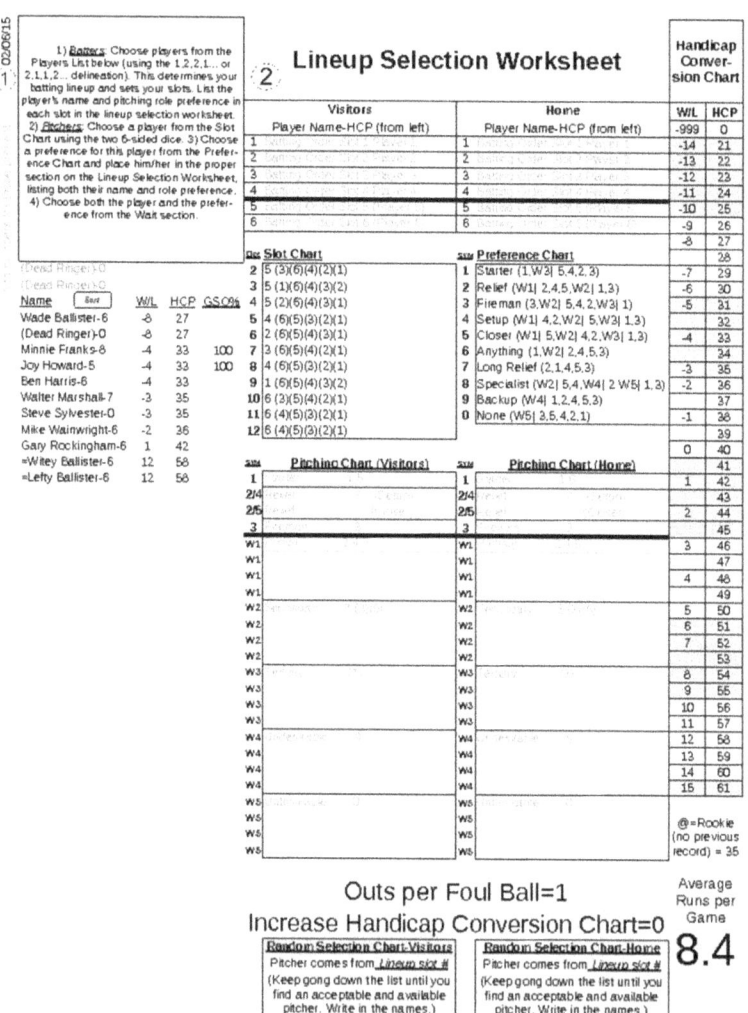

This illustration is in the public domain. You may copy it, give it to your friends, and use it for playing games, etc.

Available at: http://glorylight.org/MiBaseball_Lineup_Selection_Worksheet.pdf or http://1ref.us/lineup Have fun!

Appendix D

The Stake Out (Instructions for Setting-up the Default Lines)

Designing your ball field can compose much of the fun involved in playing any game, both in the design work itself, and for many years to come, for it can abundantly enhance your enjoyment and augment the delight of your members and guests. The old adage is still true that the more you put into something the more you generally reap from it. A poorly built field can diminish the effects of the game and crush your spirits. I recommend having a ball field that will be attractive, friendly, and maybe even idyllic. A little attention at the beginning will reap compounding rewards appropriate for a game such as this.

When building your ball field, you will need to place stakes or colored flags[137] to mark your lines temporarily. You can make these or get them at the hardware store. You may use chalk, paint, or string for drawing your lines. If you use paint or chalk, you will

---

[137] I will call them all "stakes" for our purposes. I will use the word "markers" to refer to the permanent markers you will place for use during the games. I recommend using colored flags (rags) on these markers during games to make them easier to see.

need at least 200 feet of string as a guide. You can obtain a painting machine from a local sporting goods store, or maybe your local high school or baseball league will let you borrow theirs. You can push that around and then you don't have any string to trip over. The painted lines will eventually wear away over time.

After placing the stakes and drawing your lines, you will want to embed markers in the turf. PVC plumbing caps (1½- or 2-inch caps work best). It is wise to paint each marker different colors so that you know which colored line each marker belongs to. Partially embedded PVC pipe works well for marking the batter's boxes also. It is a good idea to use some stiff wire or spikes to secure longer pipe in the ground.

For this job you will need the following supplies:

- 57[138] stakes or colored flags

- 57[139] PVC end caps normally used in plumbing (1½" or 2")

- up to 2500 feet of string, turf, or sidewalk paint, or line chalk (but only 200 feet of string if you use the paint or chalk)

- two tape measures of at least 170 feet

- spray paint for the markers; black, medium blue, red, grey (or silver), yellow, white, purple, turquoise (or light blue), and pink

- a regulation yard stick

- a hammer if you use wooden stakes

Look at the Field Plan for where to place your stakes and your lines. Then I suggest the following procedure:

1. You need to first mark a 120' by 120' square. (All measurements will be in literal feet.) Start with either the left field or right field foul line.[140] You will want to start with the foul line that is the most critical for placing, such as proximity to a house or other structure. You also want to try to have the main pitching mound, and maybe even the batter's circle, on a small rise, if possible, for drainage. For the sake of discussion, I will start with the left field foul line.

2. Place your first stake where home plate is to be set. This is "home." Stake one end of the tape measure in the ground or have someone hold it for you when making your measurements.

---

138   You will need 64 if you are not using a homerun barrier.
139   You will need 64 if you are not using a homerun barrier.
140   If possible, aligning the left field foul line due east-west seems to work fairly well. At any rate, pay attention to the alignment of the sun at different times of the day and at different times of the year. Other factors may also have an affect.

Appendix D   The Stake Out (Instructions for Setting-up the Default Lines)

3. Measure 140'[141] and place stakes at 15', 28', 33', 36', 50', 55', 75', 90', 120', and 140'. This will be your left field foul line, so pay particular attention to where it goes with respect to nearby structures or potential obstacles.

4. From your 120' left field stake, measure another 120' toward center field. Make it as close to perpendicular as possible to the left field foul line using the naked eye. Place a temporary stake there, but leave your tape measure on the ground.

5. From your home stake, use your second tape measure to measure 169' 8½" toward the newly placed centerfield marker. Then make the two tape measures cross at exactly the 120' and the 169' 8½" marks on the respective tape measures. Move the centerfield marker to that spot and place it permanently.

6. Now, from the 120' stake on the LF[142] foul line place a stake 30 feet along that line toward center field. (That will be your LLCF blue line marker.) Also from home to the center field stake, place stakes at 15', 30' 3", 31' 6", 50' 11", 65', and 84' 10½." (The latter marker marks the exact center of your square and will serve as a benchmark only.) Now you can move your tape measures.

7. From the newly placed center field stake, measure 120' toward the vicinity of the right field foul line, making it as parallel as possible to the left field foul line using the naked eye. Place a temporary stake there, but leave your tape measure on the ground.

8. From your home stake, use your second measuring tape to measure 140'[143] in the direction of the right field foul line, making it as close to perpendicular to the left field foul line as possible. Then make the two tape measures cross at exactly the 120' marks on the respective tape measures. Move the right field stake to that spot and place it semi-permanently.

9. Place a stake 90' from the center field stake toward the right field stake. This will become your RRCF blue line marker.

10. Now you can remove the tape measure that goes from the center field stake to the right field stake and use it to check your measurements. (Leave

---

141   If you have room, go ahead and extend your line to 155 feet. You may need the extra distance depending on whether you use a barrier and/or where you put it. Place a stake if you do not plan to use a barrier.

142   L=Left; C=Center; R=Right; F=Field

143   If you have room, go ahead and extend your line to 155 feet. You may need the extra distance depending on whether you use a barrier and/or where you put it. Place a stake if you do not plan to use a barrier.

your home plate-to-right field tape measure on the ground.) With the tape measure you just removed, measure the distance from the left field stake to the right field stake. It should measure very close to 169' 8½", and it should cross very close to the stake in the exact center of your square, which should also be very close to 84' 10½" mark on the tape measure. If either of these two measurements is significantly off, consider adjusting the right field stake. If there is any difference in the two possible placements of the right field stake, you may want to split the difference between the two indicated possible placements, or if the difference is significant, measure the previously placed lines again.[144]

11. When you are satisfied with the final placement of the right field stake, then place stakes at 15', 28', 33', 36', 50', 55', 75', 90', and 140' along the right field line, the 120' stake being already placed.

12. Now you have your square. It is time to draw the lines on your field, marking the four sides of your 120' square, the cross ("X") lines through the middle, and the extensions to 140' down the foul lines. You can also draw your LLCF and RRCF lines to home plate. Extend the drawing approximately 25' passed the LLCF and RRCF stakes, but do not place stakes at the end of the extensions. Use paint, chalk, or string.

13. Now it is time to place the LCF line. From home, measure 140' toward the left-center field area and make the 140' mark fall exactly on the line for the back side of the square. Place a stake in this place. Extend exactly 20' passed the LCF stake (to 160') and place a stake in this place. Also place a stake where the new line intersects the center cross line between the left field and right field stakes. Finally, place a stake at the 62' mark on the tape measure. (These stakes become the LCF blue, black, grey, and yellow line markers respectively.)

14. Do the same for the RCF line.

15. Now you can draw your LCF and RCF lines from home plate. Extend them 20' passed the LCF and RCF stakes to the black line stakes. Use paint, chalk, or string.

16. Now draw the black line all the way around from left field to right field. Place stakes where the LLCF and RRCF lines intersect the black line. I suggest you also draw the blue lines (both the corner and close lines), but the blue line drawing is not needed for staking the default lines. However,

---

144   I will let you choose your definition of "significant." Absolute perfection is not necessary, and "pretty close" should not affect the fun of playing the game.

if you build a custom black line, the blue line drawing will definitely be needed.

17. For the red line stake, start at the 75' mark on the left field foul line and measure 55' toward the center field stake. Place a stake where the 55' mark intersects the LCF line. You can now draw the red and grey lines, skipping the center field area if you want to. Place stakes where these lines intersect the LLCF line (2 places).

18. Do the same for right field.

19. You have two more stakes to place in order to finish the yellow line. From home down the LLCF line place a stake at the 55' mark.

20. Do the same for right field. Draw the yellow line all the way around.

21. Now for the white line. This line is a little more complicated, but not much. You already have the bases, so that is done. For the white line itself, please refer to the Field Plan. The white line actually skirts in front of the bases, so follow these steps:

    - Starting with the left field side (third base), measure 3' and 33' from third base toward second base and place two stakes, respectively.

    - Do the same for the right field side from first base to second base.

    - Draw the small lines that pass in front of first base, second base, and third base respectively (bypassing them). Then draw the two lines between these three lines all the way around, but do not draw these lines all the way to the bases themselves. When finished, it should look like it does on the field plan (Default Lines in the preface).

    - Now you need to place the four stakes that intersect the white line at the LLCF, LCF, RCF, and RRCF lines.

22. You don't need to draw the purple line unless you want to.

23. You do need to draw the turquoise line so you can place two stakes at the intersections of the LCF and RCF lines respectively. (You do not need stakes at the LLCF or RRCF lines.)

24. For the 15' batter's circle, place stakes at approximately 3' intervals at a 15' radius around the home stake. The circle will meet with the pink line to complete a full "circle" around home plate.

25. You also need a stake 1 foot directly behind home plate.

26. The last marker to stake is the center field orange marker. This marker is exciting and a focal point of the game. Draw a line directly between the two 160' stakes in LCF and RCF. Then run a tape measure (or string) between the centerfield stake and the 75' stake on the right field foul line and place a stake where the tape intersects the line just drawn. That is the orange line marker. You don't need to draw this line unless you want to.

27. Finally, set the batter's boxes, per the illustrated diagram below.

28. Before your first game, and while your drawing is still on the field, I recommend permanently marking some of the lines, unless you want to be replacing the painted lines every two weeks, or so. You could use partially embedded PVC pipe to permanently mark your lines, like I do with the batter's boxes. Bill Veeck used to run fire hose down the foul lines. I haven't tried that yet, but if you try it, please let me know how well that works for you. That may be the best option if a local fire department is willing to donate used fire hoses.

    - I suggest permanently marking the batter's boxes (with PVC pipe reinforced with wire embedded in the ground for security), home plate to the corners of the batter's boxes touching the foul lines (with PVC pipe), the black line (with logs, old railroad ties, or old utility poles, most of which may be donated[145]), the pink line, the batter's circle, and the foul lines using whatever works for you.

    - As mentioned earlier, I suggest permanently marking all the stake placements with PVC pipe end caps embedded in the ground and painted to match the color line they represent. The caps will survive the mower, so they don't need wire reinforcements to hold them down.

    - During the game, I place colored flags (rags) on the markers for orange, blue, red, grey, yellow, purple, turquoise, pink, and (finally) the 3 bases use bigger white flags. I use a regulation baseball plate for home plate. I will leave it up to you which markers to flag, but I highly recommend at least white flags for the bases.

29. The default lines have been placed, including the black line. If you place logs or some other type of barrier along this line, as I have done, you are finished. If you choose not to use a barrier, you should do three things:

    - Move the black line back 15 feet from the default line.

    - Make the default line the orange line.

---

145   If you really want to get fancy, I suggest you build a fence or wall.

- Decide whether you still want to keep the CF orange marker you just placed and just call that a triple area, in which case, replace the orange flag with a white flag.

However, if you want to have some fun, feel free to use a barrier (maybe a fence) and become creative with the black lines.

30. Now that's a ballfield!

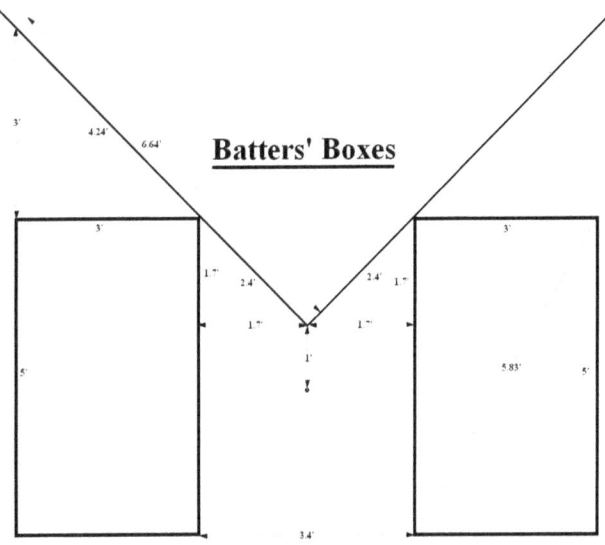

Appendix E

Oops!

(Remedial Options for Errant Play on the Field)

Every self-respecting baseball game has errors, right? Errors are just part of the game. Well, this game has errors also, but just a little different. Should either of the following options be used (live pitching versus off the tee), count a "team error" against the team in the field.[146] Score the play as you ordinarily would, but note the error. If indicated below, a second "error" can also arise during the play. Treat this "error" in the same manner as you would a walk, only it is called "1E–0" and the runners are forced. Any runs scored as a result of any errors are earned. (The only unearned runs come during the tiebreaker inning.)

- If batting against live pitching:
    - The batter can always accept the result of the play (if that can be determined), or

---

146   In miniature baseball, team errors have no effect on base runners.

- The batter can cancel the play and accept a "ball" added to his count, or
- If the batted ball was a fair ball, the batter can cancel the play and accept a one-base error (1E–0)[147] followed by a wildcard tee.

• If batting off the tee, accept the result of the play as it lies. Only if that cannot be determined or if there is interference, do you replay the swing. (Do not count another error if a swing has to be replayed.)

---

[147] Runners hold unless forced.

Index

A
Absent Batter, 23, 33, 42, **66**, 68, 69
Absent Pitcher, 38, 42, **66**, 69
Absent Player, **65**-69, 79, 84
All-Star, 67, **69**
Ambidextrous, 7, **22**, 23, 66-68, **79**-81, 83, 84
Area Criteria, **36**
At Bat, 13, **24**, 45, 58, 63, 68
Automatic Called Strike Three, 26, **64**, 66, 74, 75

B
Balk, **31**
Ball (count), **25**, 26
Base Hit, 25, **27**, 35, **36**, **37**, 41, 43, 57-62, 74, 75
Base Runners, 24, 30, **34**, 35, 37, 41, 43, 53, 60, 94
Bases, 12, 17-19, 25, 27, 28, 30, 33, 38, 49, 59, 60, 91, 92
Batter Faced Pitcher, **24**

Batter Hits the Equipment, **26**
Batter's Box, 10, **19**, 22, 27, **29**, 32, 33, 51, 66, 88, 92
Batter's Circle, **29**, 49, 88, 91, 92
Batting from the Tee, 22, 23, 24, 29, **31**-33, 35, 38, 42, 45, 62, 63, 66, 81, 94, 95
Batting Out of Turn, **44**
Black and White, **59**
Bunt, 14, 32, **35-37**

C
Challenge Season, **70**, 71
Colored Lines, **29**, 35, 59

D
Dead Ringer, **22**, 23, 33, 38-42, **65**-69, 79-81, 84
Dead Ringer and Ambidextrous Persons, 22, 23, **66**, **79**-81, 84
Dead Ringer Pitches to Himself, **66**
Default Lines, **8**, 47, 48, **87**, 90-92
Double Foul out, **37**
Double Play, 18, **36**, **37**, 38, 41, 45, 46

Index

E
Equipment, 16, **20**, 26
Errors, 18, 25, **94**, 95

F
Fair Ball, **30**
Fat Bat (orange), **22**, 32, 35
Field, **19**, **47**, **87**
Field Conflicts, **45**, **48**
Field Design, **87**-93
Field Plan, **8**, 9
Fielders, **23**, 76
Flavor of the Game, **45**
Fly Balls, **24**, 37, 54
Foul Ball, 12, **30**, 34-38, 46, 50
Foul Pole, **31**
Foul outs, **34**, 38, 48, 62, 64

G
Grass, **50**
Ground Balls, **24**, 34, 37, 38, 41, 50

H
Handicaps for Batters, 56-**59**, **60**
Handicaps for Pitchers, 56-**59**, **62**
Hit By Pitch, 32, **38**, 57

I
Improper Stance, **32**
Inning Handicap, **73**
Inside the Park, **42**

L
Lineup Selection, **66**
Lineup Selection Worksheet, **82**

O
Obstructions, **48**, **49**, 53
Orange Bat (Fat), **22**, 32, 35
Outs, **34**

P
Passed Ball, **26**, 62
Person, **22**, 23, **42**, **79**-81
Plate Appearance, **24**, 33, 66

Player, **22**, 23, 42, 53, **57**, **65**, 67, **68**, **73**, 79, 80
Player Handicap, **57**, 69, **73**, 75
Players, **22**, 53, 57, 68

Q
Quadruple Foul out, **37**, 38, 64
Quadruple Play, 35-**37**, 54, 63

R
Random Rosters, 56, 69, **71**
Random Season, **71**
Rookies, **57**, 69
Round Robin, **70**, 71
Rule Conflicts, **45**

S
Scoresheet, **59**, 67, 69, **78**
Set Rosters, **71**
Slot, **24**, 66-69
Static Version, **74**, 75
Stolen Base, **38**-41, 45
Strike (count), **25**, 26-29
Strike Zone, **25**-27, 29, 60, 62
Strike Zone Board(s), **22**, 26, 38, 41, 62, **64**, 74
Substitution, 43, 65, **67**, 69, 70

T
Tee (See "Batting from the Tee")
The Pitcher and the Batter Are the Same Actual Person, 23, **42**
Tiebreaker, 17, 25, **42**, 43, 94
Time Up, **24**, 32, 33, 38, 42, 43, 45, 57, 66-68
Triple Foul out, **37**
Triple Play, **37**, 46
Try For a Tee Shot, **32**, 66
Two-player, **22**, 25, 66, 67

W
Walk, 24, 25, 31, **33**, 34, 42, 57, 63, 66, 67
Weak (Pitcher), **33**, 34, 69
Wildcard (Tee), **32**, 63, 66, 67, 95
World Series, 12, **71**

We invite you to view the complete
selection of titles we publish at:

www.ASPECTBooks.com

scan with your mobile
device to go directly
to our website

Please write or email us your praises, reactions, or
thoughts about this or any other book we publish at:

Info@ASPECTBooks.com

ASPECT Books titles may be purchased in bulk for
educational, business, fund-raising, or sales promotional use.
For information, please e-mail:

BulkSales@ASPECTBooks.com

Finally if you are interested in seeing
your own book in print, please contact us at

publishing@ASPECTBooks.com

We would be happy to review your manuscript for free.

www.ingramcontent.com/pod-product-compliance
Lightning Source LLC
Chambersburg PA
CBHW080552170426
43195CB00016B/2768